A Journey of Grief, Gratitude, and Grace

By Ruth I. Halvorson

Kirk House Publishers
Minneapolis, Minnesota

A Journey of Grief, Gratitude, and Grace

Ruth I. Halvorson

ISBN – 13: 978-1-933794-72-3

ISBN – 10: 10933794-72-0

LCCN: 2013940375

Kirk House Publishers, PO Box 390759, Minneapolis, MN 55439

Manufactured in the United States of America

To my family, who is a presence of love and support to me in every situation

Contents

Acknowledgments

This project would not have been possible without the encouragement and generous support of John and Eleanor Yackel. Their belief in the value of this topic for others, as well as their faith in me, finally persuaded me to take on the task. Their friendship with Loren and me has spanned many years. John and Loren participated in a small men's book group for several years called "Da Guys." The conversations they shared and the books they read covered wide and diverse topics, and, as Loren said in jest, sometimes they even got around to talking about the book they read.

Perhaps Randy Nelson is most responsible for getting me started writing in the first place. Randy's invitation to present a forum at his church on grief and loss was the impetus that first got me to even think about writing on this topic.

I am also grateful to Charles Pederson, who edited my manuscript with skill and thoughtfulness and helped make the final product better. I express thanks to Daren Hastings for his book design skills and artistic eye in layout and to Mary Kaye Kuzma for her expertise in bringing the book to print. I am grateful to Mary, my daughter, for writing the foreword and for providing helpful suggestions for my manuscript, and to Mark, my son, for his photography work. Finally, I am grateful to my entire family for being a sounding board and encouraging me along the way.

Foreword

Everyone dies. All life comes to an end. New generations replace the old. Those who remain carve new chapters; their whittling knives are grief, memory, and the simple yet courageous act of stepping out into each new day. The ebb and flow of life and death is organic, expected, and sometimes even hoped for. Yet each measured life holds its own powerful story. The particular stories we carry cannot be argued or denied. They shape a life and create a winding path never before traveled. Out of any particular life, universal truths rise to the surface. As E. B. White once wrote, "Advice to young writers who want to get ahead without any annoying delays: don't write about Man, write about a man."

My mother's story is about a man—my father, and her husband for more than fifty-seven years. The journey they shared dramatically changed when treatment for my father's cancer had run its course. Yet changes in life are often circular, giving birth to new adventures. This adventure included a hospice bed, managing a boatload of medications, and learning the language of decay while straddling the mysteries of life and death.

Even in his weakened state, Dad's wit was razor sharp. I will never forget one morning. From his hospice bed, Dad was channel surfing. The selection of talk shows, infomercials, and exercise programs offered meager fare at best. Shutting the TV off, he offered this commentary: "We don't need to go to hell, we are already there." The consummate teacher, what he said was true of our culture. Always on the lookout for a pun or play on words, he provided his own comic relief.

By virtue of the proximity of my siblings and their spouses—each of us living less than five miles from our parents—we were given a gift. During the four months of hospice care, for one full day and night a week, one of us lived with them. It wasn't long before the dying process became a normal part of our daily lives. Adaptability is a human gift; being nimble and willing to learn helps us survive and thrive. We had no choice. Our dad needed hospice care, and keeping him home was our priority. In retrospect, these months with our Dad were his final gift. With him we would learn about relinquishing and letting go while opening ourselves to death's rhythm and demands. We were students in a crash course, immersed in an experiential dying lab. Finessing a catheter bag, making soft foods, and crushing pills and inserting them into the side of Dad's mouth were our new assignments.

I remember one dark evening in the season of Epiphany. As others were eating supper, I quietly slipped into my parents' bedroom and settled into the chair nearest Dad's bed. Being a Lutheran pastor, I had a sermon to craft. After attempting to write something inspirational, I set down my laptop to take a break. I found myself breathing with Dad. In and out, a pause, then a breath. Sometimes his breathing was fast and difficult to imitate. Pauses were unexpected rest notes. The act of breathing in concert with my dying father was my way of being in solidarity with him.

Throughout these pages you will read how we breathed with and sometimes for my father. It was not always easy. There were dark nights of the soul. There were squabbles and different opinions about care. Lack of sleep led to crankiness and exhaustion. Yet the journey we all shared, upon which my mother reflected every night through the online CaringBridge journal, is one I would never trade.

Perhaps the point is how we can be human together—with our questions and doubts, our opinions and feelings. Death, and the grief and remembering that follow, remind us of our humanness. This is a gift. When we love, we mourn. Grief and joy are companions on the same journey.

Mary Halvorson
May 2013

Introduction to the Journey

Endings offer new beginnings. Challenges open up new possibilities. Winter invites a new spring, and death leads to new life.

Since the death of my husband, Loren, on February 15, 2010, I have been on a journey, a road I have not traveled before. This journey has taken me along unexpected paths, to places I did not want to go, and opened up vistas that offer unexpected and surprising opportunities. From sorrow, joy slowly appears; from pain, healing begins; and from loneliness, new life emerges—the paradox of this journey.

Accompanying Loren on his final journey was a unique privilege. It offered new understanding and perspective not only about dying but also about my own journey and about life itself. This experience provided learning that could not be achieved by academic study or reading a book on the subject. Firsthand, I experienced the complex and multiple facets of dying. With Loren able to remain in hospice care in our home, the proximity of the dying process could not be avoided. It was real and raw, not glossed over, not camouflaged. Throughout this life-altering experience, I made discoveries about myself: how I reacted and responded to this new reality; how I coped with the changes, sometimes sudden and unexpected; what strengths and weaknesses I had; how strong my faith and commitment were; how willing I was to let go; how ready I was to accept my approaching new reality—living alone without my life partner.

Gone, but Still Present

Loren's physical presence is gone, but his influence and spiritual presence remain. Our relationship did not end with death, for love continues to grow in another way. At unexpected moments I feel his presence real and near—as though he were sitting right next to me. One night I was awakened from a deep sleep when I heard him call my name. "Ruthie." I raised my head off the pillow and responded as if he had just walked into the room, "Yes?" This brief encounter provided the encouragement and confidence I needed at the time to make an important decision I was facing. In another dream, I saw him riding an escalator as it ascended to the next floor where I was sitting by a table. He looked at me and smiled as though eager to see me. These fleeting encounters are infrequent, yet they bring joy, as well as encouragement. I hang on to them, and like a cozy, soft afghan, they bring comfort.

These surprising moments mysteriously help retain connection and foster love. Centuries ago, Saint John Chrysostom wrote, "They whom we love and lose are no longer where they were before. They are now wherever we are."

As a couple we had many opportunities to travel, and on different occasions we lived overseas and took delight in exploring new frontiers. Together we enjoyed nature, music, and all the joys and adventures of raising five children. We also traveled far and wide—while sitting in our living room as we read books together and engaged in long, stimulating conversations on theological and political issues, as well as social and global concerns. Later in our marriage, we teamed up in leading retreats and presenting forums and talks.

Because of these times of significant sharing and stimulating conversations, what I miss most now is companionship—someone with whom I can talk about my day when I return home or discuss important issues and concerns. I miss someone to whom I can say whatever is on my heart and know I will be heard, respected, and loved. I can still hear Loren saying, when I returned home from an event, visit, or meeting, "Sit down and tell me all about it."

CaringBridge

How have I filled the void and emptiness? Regular writing has been helpful to me. I have kept a journal and write often. In my journal I write whatever springs from my heart. It is a place I can wrestle with the big and little issues of life. This becomes a safe place. Here I can honestly express my challenges, my discouragement, my loneliness, my joys, my experiences, and my hopes. I do not strive for perfection or write for anyone else. I write solely for my own exploration, understanding, and clarification. For me, writing can help clarify matters and often soften the impact of more trying and challenging situations.

Every day during my husband's long illness, I posted entries on the CaringBridge journal, and my family also wrote occasional entries. CaringBridge is a charitable, nonprofit organization offering free personalized websites for people facing serious medical conditions. The CaringBridge site offers both a journal and a guestbook. The journal provides a link for those who are ill to write for themselves, or a place for their spouses or family members to write about the health condition of their loved ones. The guestbook provides an opportunity for friends, family, colleagues, and others to write words of love and support to the ill person and family.

Writing daily in the CaringBridge journal became a helpful and even, in some ways, a therapeutic exercise for me. I did not foresee, however, how positive and encouraging the guestbook entries would become for Loren and me. Every day until the last week of his life, Loren asked to have the entries read and, often, reread: this became a healing ritual for us. Our families' and friends' thoughtful entries offered support and comfort to us and maintained a special connection with those who wrote. CaringBridge created an unexpected experience of community; it mattered as my family and I spent many hours confined to the apartment caring for Loren. We felt a personal connection with each person who sent an entry. CaringBridge helped us keep everyone who was interested regularly informed, limiting telephone inquiries to our home—a blessing because rest times for both Loren and the family care givers were often unpredictable. The CaringBridge site remained open throughout the months of Loren's illness and continued for another six months after I had stopped writing. This is standard for the website.

The journal writing became a regular pattern that was helpful, sometimes difficult, but always a reflective part of my day. In some ways it felt like a sacred ritual. I usually found myself writing late in the evening—the dark of night drew me into a thoughtful mood. This became my special time to reflect on the day, as I attempted to express its events and draw the important lessons from it. Many evenings I was exhausted and tempted not to write. Though no one required me to write every day, something within me was not satisfied until I did, even though on some days my entry was very short. Many readers of the CaringBridge journal said they looked forward to receiving my daily updates and reflections. Others said they used the entries as a devotional or personal reflection piece. In retrospect, I can see that it became a discipline that kept me more centered and in touch with the roller coaster of my emotions.

> *From the Journal ~*
>
> *We have set up this CaringBridge site so that you might keep tabs on how Loren and Ruth are doing and so that you can send messages in the guestbook. Be assured that all messages sent will be read and appreciated.*[1]

Further Encouragement to Write

Readers of the journal and other friends encouraged me to write more extensively—apart from my CaringBridge journal—about my experience of loss and grief. This felt like a daunting challenge. Initially, I wondered how I could even interpret my feelings, let alone express them in words. My feelings and emotions were still raw and unpredictable. Yet strangely enough, I was drawn inexplicably to the task, even as I questioned my ability to accomplish what has been my most personal challenge.

---

[1] "From the Journal" extracts are from appendix A, Complete CaringBridge Journal. They appear throughout this book. They do not follow a chronological sequence of Loren's hospice experience. Rather, they illustrate the book's discussions. I recommend that you read the entire journal, which chronologically follows the ups and downs of Loren's last months.

I would not have given serious thought to writing further on this topic, even with the regular encouragement of friends and readers of the CaringBridge journal, if it were not for an invitation I received from Randy Nelson, a colleague of Loren's and a friend to both of us. Four months after Loren's death, Randy asked if I would present a forum on grief and loss at his church. The forum was to take place in two months from that time. My initial reaction was great surprise. "What do I know about grief? I have only my own experience," I exclaimed.

"That's precisely what we want," he replied. He gave me a couple of days to decide whether to accept his invitation. I said yes, not knowing where this "yes" would take me.

I had several weeks to reflect more carefully on my experience and consider ways to approach the task. Because I had made a commitment, I was compelled to write. But where would I begin? How would I begin? Even more challenging, how could I share a personal journey of grief and loss in a way that others might find helpful and meaningful? How would I interpret emotions that are often unsettled and inconsistent? How might I articulate unpredictable and erratic feelings following this major loss?

Growing from Loss

We all experience loss. This is inevitable. There are major losses and minor losses, but loss touches us all in some way. There may be the loss of a job, the breakdown of health, an unfulfilled dream, a lost opportunity, a broken relationship.

Loss by death is unavoidable. With sudden, unexpected loss or death, we deal with the tremendous shock of such a heart-rending event. At other times a death may be expected. In fact, if the person has suffered a prolonged and painful illness, it may be longed for by both the sufferer and the loved ones who witnessed the suffering. In situations where the dying process is a more extended goodbye, there is a unique opportunity to prepare with the loved one and family for the eventual physical separation. We are each affected differently, and we respond differently. How we deal with death and loss is a challenge we must face, learn to live with, and seek to grow from.

As our relationships change after a loss, so too does our outlook on life. In my case, I have become more willing to ask questions, more comfortable with entertaining doubt, more willing to speak my mind, more willing to trust my inner truth, and less certain and fixed in my answers. I am more certain about what is important, what really matters in life and brings fulfillment and happiness. I am less certain about things about which I earlier felt certain. Life is not black and white but contains shades of gray and many ambiguities.

I have found that my theology has become more basic, perhaps I could say more simplified. I do not have the same interest in exploring doctrinal differences or the nuanced distinctions in belief systems I once did. I now find meaning and sustenance in the simple truth: God is love—a love that is merciful, forgiving, welcoming, and totally inclusive. This is foundational for me and could be called my ground note. Everything good and nurturing comes from this love. It was love that created me, and it is love that sustains me and carries me throughout the days. I have no idea what life after death will be like. This remains a mystery. Yet I dare to trust this unconditional love to care for me and for those I love at the moment of death, just as I have been cared for in life. Life has been expanded and become more precious because I have walked with death.

My Own Interpretation

When I finally took pen in hand and began to put my thoughts on paper, I found the exercise not only daunting but also surprisingly helpful. It helped me clarify, name, expose, and face my experience with death in a way I may not have done, or at least may not have done so soon. I did not expect that writing, despite the challenges, would become a transforming exercise in my own grieving and healing. The reflections in this book describe my experience, interpretation, and understanding and are written from a personal faith perspective.

People hold a great diversity of beliefs, as well as no belief. Each person will experience the dying and grieving process differently. Therefore, I encourage you to take what is helpful from these pages and leave what is not. Each person is unique and carries her or his own story. I sincerely hope that by sharing my experience and reflections, I can bring you a measure of comfort and encouragement, together with a spirit of hopefulness in your grieving and the accompanying challenges of death and loss.

1 *Interruption of Illness*

My husband, Loren, died after a long, painful struggle with prostate cancer. Our marriage lasted more than 57 years and included raising a lively household of three sons and two daughters. Living with another person for more than five decades leads to an intricately intertwined and deeply rooted life together. Early on I learned how formational Loren's young adult experiences were in shaping his life and vocation.

Refugee Resettlement

Following college, Loren had an extraordinary experience that played a seminal role in the direction and shape of his life's work and passion. Immediately after graduation in 1949, a few years after the ending of World War II, Loren spent 22 months working for Lutheran World Federation (LWF) as a field representative in Germany, helping in the resettlement of primarily Baltic refugees. This experience touched him to the core. Working daily with complex immigration issues, with families and individuals uprooted from their beloved homeland and sent to foreign places, was formative and transformational for a young adult. Seeds were planted in those years that would last a lifetime. This experience evoked an interest in and dedication to the less fortunate that he never lost. Some years after graduating from theological seminary, he received a doctorate in ethics in the field of church and society.

Throughout his career, Loren focused on equipping the laity (the people) of the church. He sought to connect piety and politics, prayer and social justice, faith and service. He continued with this same focus in his retirement. Loren volunteered many hours with son Paul in working to restore and renovate homes for low-income families. He also continued to work for inclusivity for individuals and groups not fully recognized by church or society.

ARC Retreat Center

In the mid 1970s Loren joined me in realizing a dream I felt called to bring about: the ARC (action, reflection, and celebration) Retreat Center, an ecumenical center located one hour north of the Twin Cities of Minneapolis and Saint Paul. This center is a quiet place set apart for individuals and groups on spiritual journeys of renewal. It sits on 96 acres of beautiful wooded country property where no human structures had previously existed. Loren poured his energy and his creative gifts into this endeavor. Over the years the retreat center became an important part of his life. From 1978 until his retirement in 1992, Loren divided his time between the seminary and ARC, working two thirds time at the seminary and one third time at ARC. ARC was his volunteer work.

Loren enjoyed wearing different hats when at ARC. He worked primarily as maintenance man, a title he loved. He claimed maintenance work was "eternal." From the role of fixer, builder, or repairman, he moved easily into the role of seminary professor, retreat leader, preacher, or limerick writer.

These experiences prepared Loren for his ultimate life experience, dying.

Hearing the Worst and Reacting to It

Loren lived with prostate cancer, which medication had kept under control for many years. However, 7 months before his death, at a regularly scheduled visit with his urologist, it was discovered that the medication he was taking was no longer working as it had before. Further tests and x-rays were scheduled. The test results showed that the cancer had metastasized to several places in his body. The cancer was stage four, the most advanced stage. No treatment or cure was possible; no procedures, no treatments, no medications, no experimental options were available.

> *From the Journal ~*
>
> *Loren and family recently learned that his prostate cancer . . . has spread to many places in his body. . . . It has become clear that the ill effects of treatment are not worth the possible benefit.*

This was devastating. Such sudden and unsettling news took time to absorb and accept. The focus now would be solely on palliative care, or as some call it, comfort care. The goal of each day was to make Loren as comfortable and pain free as possible. The focus would be on care, not cure. The urological oncologist who gave us the news was understanding and sympathetic. Thoughtful and very patient, he gave us as much time as we needed to ask questions and take in this upsetting report. The oncologist did not leave the room until we were ready to leave.

Following the long doctor appointment, we went home. Initially, Loren had received this distressing news with outward calm and stoicism. That evening at dinner, however, Loren said he felt nauseated. Although I am not the greatest cook, his distress was about something much deeper than the quality of my cooking. We had received no ordinary news. Loren had just received a death sentence.

Loren was hit hard. The information affected every fiber of his being: physically, mentally, psychologically, and spiritually. Life would not go on as we had planned. When I look back on that day, I realize my grieving did not begin when Loren died. It began when I first heard the doctor's pronouncement, "You have stage-four cancer." Those few words altered everything, and in the blink of an eye, life changed. Nothing would be the same again. We would not be making plans for the future as we had been doing.

People may find themselves responding to upsetting news in ways they never would have anticipated. At such times people don't respond only as they think they should but in ways that are helpful and honest. For both Loren and me, growing up in Scandinavian households, strong emotions were not easily expressed. Stoicism, however, had no place now. We could not deny what was rearing up within us, nor would it be wise or healthy to do so. We needed to let our emotions have their way, in whatever way that would be. As we talked, Loren's nausea began to subside. Strong reactions may surprise us, but they are to be expected. Could it be otherwise? As human beings we instinctively want to hold on to life.

> *From the Journal ~*
> *We know this is a time of relinquishment and letting go. To a once active, passionate man, this is not always easy.*

Doubt, Faith, and Fear

We are human and possess human emotions and frailties. At life-jolting moments, we may temporarily lose sight of what can hold us together. We do not always think clearly, and the emotions we exhibit may surprise us and even seem out of character. In these vulnerable times, fear raises its head, doubts creep in, and difficult questions arise. This is normal.

Our beliefs and our faith may feel jeopardized, as well. When what we have held on to seems threatened, everything may seem threatened. What can provide that anchor for us now?

In my experience and understanding, faith is not rigid, faith is not fixed or unyielding—rather, faith is something growing, moving, changing, held deep within the heart and soul of a person. When beliefs remain rigid and inflexible, there is no room for transformation. Faith is not outside our pain and grief, but deeply held faith lifts our sagging spirits and helps bring understanding and acceptance of our pain and grief.

Faith encourages our questions, invites our doubts, receives our anger, and recognizes our pain. As Franciscan priest Richard Rohr wrote, "Faith is not first of all for overcoming obstacles; it is for experiencing them—all the way through!" Faith encourages our questions and doubts to help us experience more deeply, enabling us to move on.

Fear can be debilitating and paralyzing; it can also motivate and inspire. After a long and helpful conversation that first evening, Loren and I decided to find ways to shape the remaining time we had together as creatively as possible. Fear would not have the last word. We did not want fear to control our life.

> *From the Journal ~*
> *The Isaiah text for today [Isaiah 43:1–2,5] is very beautiful and gives much assurance and comfort . . . : "Do not fear, for I have redeemed you; / I have called you by name, you are mine. . . . / Do not fear, for I am with you. . . ."*

When we directly faced the breakdown moment, the moment of hearing the devastating news of stage-four, untreatable cancer, we were paradoxically led to a "break-open" moment; fear was disarmed and its power subdued (at least in large part). Walking so closely with death was an unfamiliar journey, and we had no detailed roadmap or directions to follow. This would be a journey that would unfold and be revealed with greater clarity and confidence with each step we took. An insightful quote from Antonio Machado, Spanish poet and playwright, expressed the reality of our journey, "Traveler, there is no path, paths are made by walking."

Paradoxically, the breakdown moment opened us to another way of responding, to a more profound understanding of our new reality. With Loren's death sentence, our priorities shifted quickly to the essentials—to what really mattered: relationships and family. What previously had seemed so important no longer was so significant. Now death was knocking at our door. Life became more deliberate and intentional. How well we could live in the present moment and face our new reality would test our faith, our creativity, and our coping capacities. Knowingly facing death can be a sad and distressing time. It can feel like an unwelcome intrusion; however, we exercised some control in how we faced each day and with what kind of attitude we developed.

> *From the Journal ~*
>
> *While holding my dad's hand, he shared with me: "I'm not waiting for heaven; I'm experiencing it right now. The amazing thing is that it isn't something new, but something old and familiar and very warm."*
>
> *—Mark (child #2)*

Loren and I decided early on we would make an effort to transform the time from dread to delight, from fear to joy, striving to make the most of the time we had.

Three Cups of Tea

On most mornings in retirement, Loren and I observed a practice of reading aloud to each other and reserving time for silence and reflection. We took turns as the reader. It was surprising how many books we read by reading only 20 to 30 minutes each day. The readings often sparked ideas and long conversations.

Having just read Greg Mortenson's book entitled *Three Cups of Tea,* we got the idea to invite friends to our home for our own "three cups of tea." The notion of sharing tea with close friends in our home became a metaphor for relationships and intimate sharing. We wanted to demonstrate that life lurks in death. This was a concept Loren said he had formalized academically, but he had not understood its deeper meaning until then. Clarity of understanding often surprises one at these ultimate moments. Through these more intimate visits with friends, we wanted to demonstrate that life can be enhanced even in the face of impending death.

> *From the Journal ~*
>
> *[Mom] came out to a waiting cup of hot tea with Mary and me to sit in front of the picture window looking out on Lake Superior. At that moment, right before us was a full blazing rainbow. . . . Mom said, "I know all will be well." —Becky (child #4)*

The visits lifted our spirits immensely. We were amazed at how quickly we arrived at deep, heart-connecting conversations. These visits had a quality of real-ness, intimacy, and trust. How unfortunate that we too rarely arrive at such soul-filled conversations in ordinary times.

Our experience of inviting friends for tea provided dear and memorable occasions. They lasted, however, only a short time. After only four or five visits, Loren's illness and weakness began to take hold, and the days became unpredictable and difficult to plan. We had to stop our planned visits over tea. We did not know if any particular day would be good or not so good.

Talking It Over with Family

Early on, we realized it was important for the entire family to come together to talk about the changes taking place and the plans we needed to make. Our five children—Paul; Mark and spouse Lisa; Mary and spouse Dan; Becky and spouse Dan; Joel and spouse Carol—all live in the Twin Cities.

One evening, they and two or three of our seven grandchildren gathered in our living room, encircling Loren. He began to talk. His concerns focused first on what he envisioned he and we could still do to bring about greater awareness of the existing social justice issues and thereby influence social change. He also seemed concerned as to what legacy he would leave. As a family, we were confused; we did not expect this response and wondered about his concerns. It was not what we had expected to hear. Was he too centered on himself? Did he feel his work was not finished?

After reflecting a great deal on his comments, I now understand his concern quite differently. Loren was keenly aware his time on earth was limited. I believe this became a personal assessment-taking time for him. When end of life draws near, we need to be reassured that our life has mattered, that it has counted for something. We may ask ourselves: Have I used the opportunities presented to me? Is there still something I can do? Am I leaving the world a better place? Rather than being self-centered, these are realistic questions we might each ask at such a critical juncture in life.

As a family, our responsibility was to reassure Loren his work was complete. His wisdom and influence were already instilled in the hearts and lives of his family, friends, and colleagues, as well as in the hearts of hundreds of students he had taught over three decades in parishes, the seminary, retreats, seminars, and conferences. Gary Koutsopoulos, a seminary student of Loren's from 1993, summed up that influence: "Professor Halvorson was a man of great vision, peace, and commitment to the community. He foresaw the need of pastors to one day be 'worker/priests' both in partnership with all humankind and in affinity for those who practiced their lives, faith, and vocations in one humble movement. I will never forget the grace and empowerment of this beloved teacher."

It was enough. The only remaining work Loren had left was the hard work of dying, which is more than just the physical event of dying itself. Dying engages every aspect of who a person is—the psyche, the spirit, the emotions, the letting go, the goodbyes. All of life comes crashing in and seeks resolution. We his family were there to help him do that as well as possible. We assured him we would accompany him all the way. He would not be alone. We were there to give support, comfort, and physical and spiritual care and to try to bring a measure of joy to each day.

Unsuccessful Radiation Treatments

A series of thirty radiation treatments was prescribed by the radiation oncologist after we learned that Loren's cancer had spread. Although the cancer had spread from his prostate to other places in his body, the hoped-for result of these treatments was that the radiation would shrink the enlarged prostate tumor and relieve the pressure and buildup of pain Loren was experiencing more and more. The pain, however, was controlled by medication that provided him relief.

The first radiation appointments went without incident. By midpoint in the series, however, the side effects became more manifest with each treatment. We had been told, initially, that other than extreme tiredness, we could expect a more or less uneventful course of treatments. This is true for many people. Unfortunately, it was not working for Loren. He experienced more discomfort from the growing prostate tumor, along with some bleeding. We talked with Loren's primary physician, Alden, a family physician and friend, as well as with our daughter-in-law Lisa, also a physician. We learned that the hoped-for outcome would not take effect for another several months and possibly not before a year, if at all. This questionable outcome and the growing discomfort and pain made both doctors agree that continuing the treatments was inadvisable. The radiation oncologist was disappointed with our decision to stop and strongly encouraged us to continue for at least a few more treatments.

It was difficult to challenge medical expertise, yet it became increasingly clear to us who witnessed Loren's growing distress that it was more compassionate and caring to focus on his physical well-being than on his disease. Compassion was more important than cure when no cure was possible.

Investigating Hospice Care

As Loren's energy continued to wane and his body weaken, our efforts focused primarily on keeping him comfortable, managing his pain, and finding creative ways to provide as much quality of life as possible in each day. Two suggestions our daughter-in-law Lisa made that I had not considered were to begin hospice care and to open a CaringBridge website to keep family and friends informed. My knowledge and understanding of both hospice care and CaringBridge were minimal. My first response was that we didn't need those services yet; it was premature to tap into these resources. Both suggestions implied to me an immediate finality—but how timely and right both suggestions proved to be. I now understand the importance of having support and resources along the journey, as well as at the end.

Like a student enrolled in a new class, I started to learn about hospice care. Deciding which program to choose among the many offered was challenging. My decision to go with the Fairview Hospice Program was primarily because of their nearby location and the services they offered. We began with a helpful 2-hour home visit from a hospice nurse and a social worker. They carefully explained all the benefits and services their program offered.

Their hospice program provides home visits from nurses, doctors, home health aides, massage therapists, music therapists, and chaplains. Hospice care can also be provided in other nonhome settings such as in some hospitals and nursing homes or designated hospice homes. Hospice also provides trained volunteers who, upon request, will regularly visit to offer friendship and care for a period of 2 to 3 hours at a time. This provides needed respite for the primary care givers to rest, attend a concert, go for a walk, visit a friend, or whatever would offer a change of pace. As a family we decided to care for Loren in our home with hospice services brought into the intimacy of our private lives.

Because the family had decided not to seek any further medical treatment, hospice care became possible. Hospice is available only when medical treatment is no longer being pursued. Our home hospice service was covered through the Medicare insurance program. This was an enormous financial help. This coverage is determined when the primary doctor and the hospice medical director certify that the patient is terminally ill with an expectation of 6 months or less to live and with services provided by a Medicare-approved hospice program. It seemed that entering home hospice care for Loren was the right course to take, and Loren agreed.

To provide hospice services in the home, the provider requires that separate arrangements be made for 24/7 patient care. Hospice does not provide the daily hands-on care. Because hiring outside 24-hour nursing care is very costly, my family agreed to help provide that care. I am fortunate that all five of our children and spouses live in the Twin Cities and not too distant from me. A rotation schedule was set up, with a different family member coming every 24 hours. Realistically, family home care is not possible for every hospice patient. The hospice patient may not have family, or family members may be scattered geographically. They may be unable to arrange work schedules or simply be uncomfortable with providing hands-on care to the dying.

Soon we entered the rhythm of regular hospice visits that provided counsel, ordering and management of medications, and instruction on good care giving. Hospice is a philosophy of care that focuses on palliative or comfort care rather than on curative treatment of a terminally ill person. The hospice philosophy believes the quality of life is as important as the length of life. Hospice treats the person, not the disease. No medical treatments, tests, or procedures are prescribed when in hospice care. The overall goal is to control pain, provide as much quality of life as possible in the final stages of illness, and finally allow the patient to die with dignity.

Wonderful Hospice Staff Members

Jean, the primary nurse assigned to Loren, paid a visit to our home twice a week. Later in Loren's illness, she came three times a week. She was the nurse we saw most regularly; however, other nurses came when Jean was off duty or unable to come.

With each visit, the nurse assessed the situation, checked medications for their effectiveness, ordered prescriptions, and at times ordered medical equipment that would be beneficial. The first delivery was a hospital bed. This required rearranging our bedroom to make room for it. Later a large, comfortable lift/recliner chair with electric motor to lift a person into standing position was delivered to our home. The nurse answered our questions and gave helpful instructions and tips on how to attend to each situation. She also prepared us for what to expect in the days ahead. Donretha, the home health aide assigned to Loren, also came two times each week in the beginning and later three times each week. She assisted with Loren's baths and attended to all his personal care needs. Home health aides are not nurses, but they are skilled in what they do. Donretha and those who came as her occasional replacement provided great comfort and relaxation to Loren.

Music therapist Janelle came once every two to three weeks, bringing with her a portable keyboard. As Loren lay in his bed, Janelle sang and played soft, gentle music. Her lovely voice and calming music brought both joy and relaxation.

The massage therapist visits were less frequent; however, they also provided great relaxation and soothing touch. When Loren was first asked if he would like a massage, he said, "No, I don't think so." He had never experienced a massage before. After the first trial massage, however, he became a convert. The relaxation each therapist brought to Loren usually ended with him falling asleep—a testimony to the therapists' skills.

Chaplain visits were not standard practice, but when Loren was more agitated and anxious, our nurse, Jean, arranged for Steve, the Fairview Hospice Program chaplain, to pay a visit. These visits were again instructive, calming, and supportive.

It was especially reassuring to know that whenever a challenging situation came up, hospice help was just a telephone call away any time of the day or night. I made several middle-of-the-night calls for help. Calmly and expertly the on-call hospice nurse carefully walked us through the steps we should take. If the situation was more challenging than could be adequately handled over the phone, she or someone from the hospice program made a home visit no matter the time.

Learning by Trial and Error

Even though I was present throughout Loren's confinement and witnessed his dying, I cannot articulate fully what the dying experience is like. Dying is a personal and unique experience. I do know it takes energy and work. In the ensuing weeks and months, we witnessed how true that would be—how draining and all-consuming some days were. During that time we experienced the full range of human emotions. With all the ups and downs and unpredictability of some days, we were riding an emotional roller coaster.

There were days of joy and brightness, days of bleakness and discouragement, days that were very good and seemed almost normal, and days that were troublesome. There were days when heavy, dark thoughts crept in, and days of sharing stories and wonderful memories. Sprinkled throughout all the days was Loren's unique wit and humor.

In the early weeks of Loren's illness, before hospice was arranged and regular family assistance was scheduled, I experienced days of complete exhaustion. I mistakenly thought I could care for Loren by myself. This not only was unwise and foolhardy, but it also landed me in the hospital. During intense care giving times, adequate rest and proper nourishment, as well as occasional diversionary opportunities away from the constancy of care, are essential in order to be fully present and available to the one who is ill. It is well to remember that one cannot care for the sick and dying if one does not first care for oneself. It is said it takes a village to raise a child; I experienced that it takes an extended family or community of people to care for an extremely ill person at home.

> *From the Journal ~*
>
> *Ruth visited the doctor. . . . [He] encouraged her to spend one night in the hospital for observation. —Joel (Child #5)*

The generous assistance and commitment of my family in providing around-the-clock home care was not only extremely helpful to me personally, but it also was especially meaningful to Loren to be cared for by his own family. To have each child, daughter-in-law, and son-in-law, as well as grandchildren, participate so willingly and with such strength and love, was a special grace. In addition, the benefits and gifts received by each family member outweighed the challenges, exhaustion, disruption of schedules, and sacrifices.

Medications provided another area where I had to learn by trial and error. One medication does not necessarily provide the same results for each person. Some people respond favorably and beneficially to a certain drug while others react strongly and adversely to the same drug. Loren's pain increased as his cancer progressed. His added pain led to heightened anxiety and agitation. Some of the medications given to manage the increased pain and anxiety led at times to confusion, hallucinations, and paranoia—upsetting for us to watch in a person known for his gentle spirit and even temperament.

Medications that effectively dealt with one problem often induced or heightened another difficulty. The medical team tried very hard to determine the right medication and the right dosage for the situation at hand. The effectiveness and outcome of increasing or decreasing dosages or changing a medication cannot be determined as quickly as one would like. As a result, during troubling days, Loren said he felt like he was being experimented upon. We tried to reassure him that was not the case; however, I can well imagine that the confusing and perplexing experience he was having within his body felt that way—a bewildering time for him.

> *From the Journal ~*
>
> *He developed serious pain, confusion, and unsettledness, which required more medication.*

The Dying Process

We cannot hasten or delay the hour of death. We are not in charge. In the dying process we are drawn—and sometimes even pulled—inexorably along the path of dying. Some may travel with less resistance than others. When one is knowingly approaching death, I can imagine that life itself is viewed from another perspective that others not on that journey can understand. For Loren it appeared he was little by little eliminating, purging those things that were not necessary for his final journey.

Learning about the dying process was an ongoing education for the family and me. We learned helpful information and useful tips with every visit the hospice professionals made. We also learned significantly from our own hands-on care. We learned what worked and what did not, what made Loren comfortable and what did not, what little things brought joy and comfort and what did not. Our daily accompaniment of Loren on his final journey affected each of us.

We learned that the dying person often sees a different reality. We were encouraged to validate and go along with whatever Loren said (or saw) and not try to correct him or reorient him.

Losing one's independence and the ability to take care of personal needs can bring about a feeling of helplessness and discouragement. As Loren grew weaker and more frail, he became less able to do things for himself. The realization he was losing control was troubling for him. Simple, personal care duties became more difficult to manage; he required more and more assistance. It was important for us to remind him of the things he still did control. Another important reminder to us was to always include Loren in any decisions being considered on his behalf. The ill must be kept informed regarding any procedures, practices, or changes being considered and know that they still retain a voice in the decisions made if they are able.

Unexpected Gifts

At times during his process of dying, Loren spoke very poignant words; at other times his words were confusing, and still at other times words were spoken from a reality that we did not know or understand but could only affirm.

There were also many memorable, tender, and precious moments, such as the time he said to me, "Have I told you today that I love you?"

I said, "No, but you have told me a thousand times before that you love me."

"But have I told you today that I love, you?"

"No," I said, "not today."

"I love you, Ruthie."

Another morning I leaned over his bed and said, "I love you, Sweetheart."

He responded very softly, "I love you too. You said it first, but I thought it first."

Our daughter-in-law Lisa, sitting at his bedside, once asked Loren if he had any words to describe how he was feeling. His insightful response left us amazed and pondering: "Suspended in grace and dependent on love." These words became a mantra for me.

During this time we received a beautiful blessing service from a friend, entitled, "Blessing of One Who Draws Near to Death." We discussed with Loren if he would like us to share this service with him. He said he would. The service seemed right and timely. Our entire family gathered one evening around Loren's bed. In this service, with each member participating, we shared our love and gratitude. We spoke words that would free him to take leave of us as his time drew near, and as we touched his body, we blessed his head, his eyes, his ears, his mouth, his hands, his feet, and his heart. Each part of the blessing service ended with, "You will always be a part of our hearts. Go in peace." This tender moment concluded as the family encircled his bed, holding hands, to sing the blessing sung to all guests when they leave the ARC Retreat Center: "May the long-time sun shine upon you, all love surround you, and the pure light within you guide you on your way home." As the service drew to a close, Loren raised his hand and said, "Good-bye my beloved family. I love you all very much." We will long remember that sacred moment.

> *From the Journal ~*
>
> *There is a sensitivity of seeing and hearing that goes beyond what we can know or fully understand. Clearly it is a journey—the process and planning of moving from one place to another.*

Loren received another beautiful and unexpected gift. One morning Brenda and David Mickens, a couple we had come to know at our church, Gloria Dei Lutheran Church, located in Saint Paul, presented a concert in our home. They are professional violinists. Brenda is a member of the nationally acclaimed Saint Paul Chamber Orchestra, and David plays with other professional music groups and teaches violin. They frequently share their musical gifts in special concerts and in worship at our church.

The scheduled day of the concert took place when I was in the hospital for exhaustion and to undergo a series of tests. The concert contained a rich variety of classical music and brought enormous joy to Loren, a devotee of the genre. I also enjoyed the magnificent music, listening on the telephone from my hospital bed.

From the Journal ~

Today Loren and Ruth (via phone from her hospital bed) enjoyed a home concert given by Brenda and David, two friends who are violinists. . . .
—Paul (child #1)

Another gift arrived during Loren's illness. Our grandson Jonathan wondered how he could best remember Grandpa. It was difficult for him to see his grandfather looking thin and gaunt toward the end of his life. Jonathan did not want to remember his grandfather that way. An idea came to him on one of his visits. With his cell phone, he took a picture of Loren's folded hands unbeknownst to either Loren or me. How fitting this gesture was, because Loren was a man who loved to work with his hands—building, teaching, creating, repairing, cross-stitching. On Father's Day, four months after Loren's death, Jonathan presented me with a beautifully matted and framed picture of Loren's folded hands. This he had done completely on his own. What a great and wonderful surprise. I was deeply touched. The picture represented how Jonathan would remember his Grandpa. It now hangs just beneath a more formal picture of Loren in my bedroom. The picture inspired me to write a poem about hands, Loren's hands.

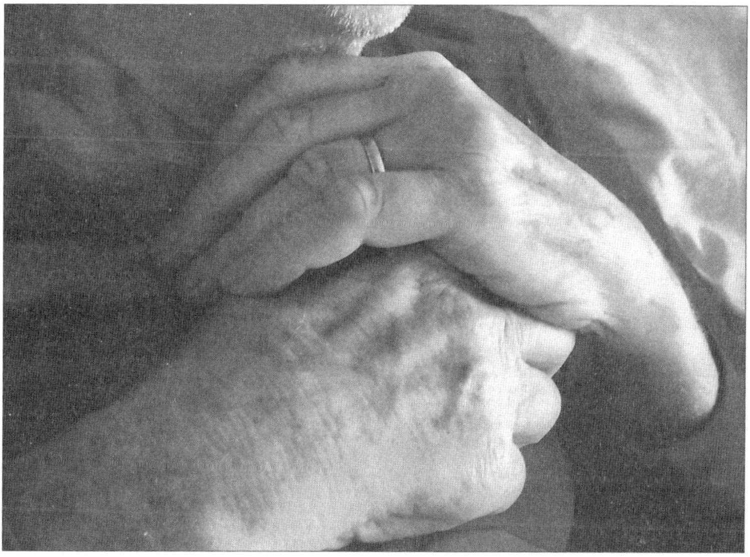

Hands That Loved and Served

Hands that loved, cared, and comforted.
Hands that wrote countless sermons, lectures, and limericks.
Hands that instructed, explained, and clarified.
Hands that guided, directed, and challenged.
Hands that designed, assembled, and produced.
Hands that sawed, measured, and built.
Hands that repaired, replaced, and restored.
Hands that glued, epoxied, and reconstructed.
Hands that wired, taped, and made things work.
Hands that remade, refurbished, and recycled.
Hands that drove tractors, lawn mowers, and trucks.
Hands that chain sawed, dug wells, and cleared land.
Hands that carefully cross-stitched and created masterpieces.
Hands that played "hokey-pokey," had fun, and invited laughter.
Hands that told stories, taught "finger exercises," conducted "bear hunts."

Hands that received, greeted, and welcomed.
Hands that prayed, anointed, and healed.
Hands that never removed a wedding band in 57 years.
Hands symbolic of tenderness, commitment, and love.
Hands that made an imprint on each child's heart and home.
Hands that connected lives, encouraged lives, touched lives.
Hands of dexterity, hands of integrity, hands of service.
Hands lined, wrinkled, and beautiful.
Hands captured on camera, a gift for us all.

Seizing the Moments

It is important for the dying to know that they are deeply loved, as well as graciously released. We often whispered in Loren's ear that we loved him and we would miss him terribly. We also told him we were ready to release him into the arms of a welcoming God.

We had an extended time with Loren, which earlier we thought we would not have. This provided opportunity to talk and share in ways we likely would never have done so intentionally and significantly in ordinary times. Loren requested a personal talk with each child, daughter- and son-in-law, grandchild, sibling, and sibling-in-law. These were important and memorable moments to share more deeply and in ways perhaps not done before. These were serious, joyful, humorous, emotional, and sacred moments—all gifts to us. At times the conversations led to fits of laughter, as well as the shedding of tears. The extended time allowed for not only one talk, especially with the children and grandchildren, but many personal talks. Loren and I also had opportunity for much deep sharing. This left me with a feeling of completeness, of nothing important left unsaid or unfinished. This sense of completeness has played a positive role in my grieving and has helped me not to look back with regret—truly a gift of grace.

Amazing Comebacks

Loren's resilience was amazing. There were many days, from our observation and care of him, that we felt would be his last day, only to be surprised again and again by a remarkable comeback of strength and alertness. This was a wonder not only to us but also to the hospice professionals. He seemed to have a storehouse of energy, alertness, and presence.

Loren's comebacks were particularly remarkable because in his last weeks, his diet consisted of anything that appealed to him, not necessarily what was most healthful. For example his food intake for many weeks consisted only of very small amounts of a 7up-and-orange-juice mix and an occasional small, juice-glass size of Dairy Queen ice cream mixed with skim milk to make what he called a "malted milk."

Trying to Figure Out Death

It is interesting to note that even in the dying process, we humans try to figure things out. This was certainly true for Loren. He had a natural curiosity and penchant to know how things work. He had always had an inquiring mind and a high degree of curiosity; that spirit had not diminished. On days when he was more alert, Loren would try to figure out what was going on in his body and in his dying process. He would begin many comments with, "I wonder if . . .," "I wonder what . . .," "I wonder when . . .," "I wonder how . . . it will be." "I wonder if time will be understood after we die in a way we cannot imagine now. Will we enter eternity simultaneously with everyone else—nobody missing—no separation?" He was ready to die and would often ask God why his dying was taking so long. He understood that the day and the hour were not his choosing; nevertheless, his questioning persisted. Perhaps just sharing these existential questions with us was helpful to his active mind. Possibly he was living the question or living his way into the answer as Rainer Maria Rilke wrote in *Letters to a Young Poet*:

> Be patient toward all that is unsolved in your heart and try to love the questions themselves, like locked rooms and like books that are now written in a very foreign tongue. Do not seek the answers, which cannot be given you because you would not be able to live them. And the point is, to live everything. Live the question now. Perhaps you will then gradually, without noticing it, live along some distant day into the answer.

Closer to the end, Loren articulated aspects of dying and living that amazed us and left us pondering. Do the dying experience living in two worlds that bring forth thoughts and comments that cannot be fully understood by those not living in that reality? Do the dying hear, see, and experience dimensions of the "life beyond" that are inaccessible to those further removed from death? There seemed to be moments when Loren made real connections with the divine. The veil between this life and the life to come became thin. There were moments when it appeared he had flashes of something beyond the ordinary, something beautiful, perhaps a foretaste of things to come. In one conversation with daughter Mary, Loren said matter of factly, "The Mystery is becoming more familiar." With many of his comments, it felt like an intrusion for me to ask for further explanation or clarification. These moments felt sacred and holy, and my questioning seemed inappropriate. As time goes by, his comments have grown in depth and meaning for me.

Loren had a long and significant career in academia, preaching, and teaching theological and spiritual matters.

He functioned to a large degree in his head. Now he was slowly making the journey from his head to his heart. This would be the shortest journey distance-wise, yet it can be the longest and most difficult journey to travel spiritually and emotionally. It means a complete letting go, a relinquishment of all we have hung on to and clung to. He understood that his work on earth was complete, and he was moving inexorably toward his final moment. His focus became centered on the journey of the heart, his home-going work, readying himself to encounter the mystery even as he was already fully known and understood by his Creator God.

> *From the Journal ~*
>
> *We pray for patience for Loren and a spirit of love and gentleness for each of us in the family as we accompany him as far as we can.*

A Different Perspective on Death

During their regular visits, the hospice personnel not only competently and compassionately attended and counseled Loren, but they also understood our needs and counseled us as a family. They spoke candidly about dying. Death was not camouflaged. Conversations about dying were natural for them and as a result became easier and more natural for my family and me. In our culture, death is often viewed as the enemy. I did not view death as the enemy, but neither did I view death as friendly. The hospice staff helped me to more graciously receive death as belonging to life, a natural part of the life cycle. Death became less foreign, less forbidding and slowly began to take on a friendlier face.

From the Journal ~

In these weeks of keeping vigil with Loren, death has taken on a different face—a face more welcoming and less foreboding, more gracious and less fearful, more natural and less frightening.

We looked forward to each visit from the different hospice personnel. They became friends. Their visits were personal and unhurried, yet always professional. We could ask any question and share any concern with them. They were highly experienced with a thorough knowledge of their work. Their visits left us feeling more confident and able to handle whatever came up.

The joyful spirit with which they worked intrigued me. I asked a few of them what attracted them to a career in hospice work. They all gave a similar answer. It was a calling. Hospice care was work they felt drawn to. Preparation for hospice work requires many years in the health care field gaining experience. During these years of varied experiences, they recognized that hospice work was what they felt most drawn to do. As one nurse said, "I love hospice work. I wouldn't last three days in a pediatrics department."

Loren and I and our children had first talked about death and our wishes many years before when Loren's father had died. He was the first of our parents to die. At that time each of us in the family wrote a brief directive as to what we wanted to happen upon our death. Even though we still had these papers, we had not reviewed our decisions or talked significantly about this topic again as a family until now, 35 years later. Our children were middle aged, engaged in their professions and raising families of their own. How did each of us in the family feel now about the directives we had written more than three decades earlier? Had our wishes changed?

Death will come to us all. As with any major life event, we can prepare for it. To talk with family, spouse, or partner about end-of-life issues is an important conversation to have. This can be challenging, but it need not be morbid when we understand death as part of the life cycle. Both end-of-life plans and advance health care directives are important and helpful information for the family. With these directives we can spell out the measures we want taken and those measures we want to avoid in a serious health event, accident, or end of life. A health care directive should also be given to our personal physicians to ensure that our wishes are known by them and will be carried out. It is important to have the directives written down, signed, and kept where family members can easily access them. Having one's specific wishes spelled out can be of enormous help and consolation to the family.

Death is a subject many avoid; articulate people who otherwise are great conversationalists often become mute when this topic comes up. We are uncomfortable with a conversation on death, especially when it involves our loved ones or ourselves. It seems threatening and frightening. With the reality of death facing my family every day in our home, it became a matter to seriously consider again. Experiencing the ease of the hospice personnel as they talked about death helped make the topic easier for us to talk about. We began by sharing what we wanted and what we thought most appropriate in keeping with our values and faith. The gifts and resources within our family— clergy, social workers, teachers, counselors—were helpful. There are many resources and books, as well as counselors, available to help individuals and families develop directives that are right and appropriate for them.

As a culture, we prepare deliberately, and sometimes elaborately, for the birth of a child—the time we enter this world. We do not place the same importance or urgency in planning regarding our own eventual death—the time when we leave this world. In its own way, the dying process becomes a "birthing" process: a birthing of new understanding, new acceptance, and new life. Both dying and birthing are hard work, and in my faith tradition, both lead to new life.

However, to accept that death is part of life does not miraculously take away the sting and pain of death or the awful emptiness and loneliness following death. A loved one is no longer physically present. Walking daily with death those many months did change my perspective and alter my attitude. Having been gently led into a richer and more profound understanding of dying itself has helped me to face life more positively and realistically since Loren's death. This was another grace afforded me in my grieving and healing. The pain of loss leaves an unmistakable ache in my heart; the attitude I seek to embrace now, however, plays a tremendously important role in my ability to move on.

Learning to Die Well

The hospice professionals said again and again that their principal purpose was to help the dying die well and with dignity. As a family this was also our purpose. We made every effort to keep Loren comfortable and his pain under control. We also sought creative ways to enrich his day. Among his many interests, Loren enjoyed documentaries and historical books. Son Mark perused the local library documentaries and checked out several videos for his father. Although initially Loren showed interest, as the cancer progressed, his energy and ability to focus waned. There were days when the capacity to enjoy was entirely lacking.

During Loren's illness, the importance of human touch took on new significance. Whether a family member, a friend, or a colleague was present, Loren would often say, "Would you hold my hand?" Touch communicates. Touch connects. Touch transcends words. Touch says, "You are not alone." Words are not always spoken or even necessary when touch is present. Eric, a friend, called one day saying he would like to come and sit with Loren, hold his hand, and simply be in silence with him. That is what he did. This remains for me a beautiful memory of compassion and love and an example of learning to die well.

Loren was always open to learning and exploring new and creative ideas. It occurred to me that what he experienced during his dying was perhaps his most significant and insightful learning. This time seemed to usher him into a new and deeper understanding of both life and death. He frequently made short comments such as, "The best word is often hidden in the last word. The most beautiful is often found in the terrible—the trying times."

> *From the Journal ~*
>
> *There is no need to rush, to go someplace else.*
> *Eternity is now. Heaven and earth are intertwined.*
> *—Mary (child #3)*

On another day Loren said, "I have taken the first step."

"How did it go?" I asked.

"It went very well," he responded.

On another morning he said, "I hear you Ruthie. I let you go and give you away to the whole world."

On a more troubling evening for Loren, our daughter Mary read William Blake's beautiful poem "The Lamb" to him.

Little Lamb, who made thee?
Dost thou know who made thee?
Gave thee life, and bid thee feed
By the stream and o'er the mead;
Gave thee clothing of delight,
Softest clothing, woolly, bright;
Gave thee such a tender voice,
Making all the vales rejoice?
Little Lamb, who made thee?
Dost thou know who made thee?

Little Lamb, I'll tell thee,
Little Lamb, I'll tell thee:
He is callèd by thy name,
For he calls himself a Lamb.
He is meek, and he is mild;
He became a little child.
I a child, and thou a lamb.
We are callèd by his name.
Little Lamb, God bless thee!
Little Lamb, God bless thee!

Following the reading of the poem, Loren's spirits brightened and with a twinkle in his eye, he said, "I have a job for you, Mary—collect all the theological books and condense them into a few poems."

With a bit of absurdity, as well as intended seriousness, Loren hinted that a few words of poetry can often convey greater truth and insight than volumes of words.

> *From the Journal ~*
>
> *This morning I read him the poem "Little Lamb," by William Blake. . . . He said, "Mary, I have a job for you. Collect all the theological books you can and condense their material into poetry." "I'm on it, Dad," I dutifully replied. —Mary (child # 3)*

Nearing Death

Loren's body continued to weaken. We could see in early February that death was near. Contrary to previous times when we had thought death was imminent, this was different. The hospice staff prepared us for the changes we would see and how best to deal with each new development. They described the last days of life as "active dying."

In the last days, Loren ingested nothing by mouth, his urine output dwindled, he was sleeping more and responding less, there were changes in his breathing patterns, and his extremities felt cool to the touch and looked more bluish. The body was shutting down.

> *From the Journal ~*
>
> *. . . With food intake having been almost nil for Loren these past couple of months or more, he is drawing from his stored reserves to keep his body going and mind active.*

Throughout these months I participated directly with the hands-on care of Loren together with another family member. Two people were needed to turn, change, and lift him up in bed. During Loren's confinement, I chose to be the primary care giver. I was the consistent one who teamed up with one of the family. However, the last two days of Loren's life were difficult for me. I had been strong throughout the past months, responding to each new stage of the dying process. Now my emotional strength was depleted. I was emotionally not able to continue to do all the tasks, large and small, that I had done up to that point. My children understood and stepped in to take my place.

Preparing Before the End

I cannot overemphasize the importance of attending to as many details and end-of-life responsibilities as possible before death. Even though we may know death is near, when it comes, we are not as capable of making clear decisions and choices as we may think. A great burden is removed from family members when as many arrangements as possible are taken care of in advance.

During the final days, we began planning a memorial service for Loren. Weeks earlier, I had asked Loren if he would like to prepare his own funeral service or at least tell us what he would like to have included. He said he trusted us, his family, to plan a beautiful service; he did not want to plan it.

He did request that the service be a "celebration of life." We selected biblical texts, hymns, and special music and determined who would give tributes and who would be assigned other tasks. We wanted the celebration of life service to reflect Loren's life, as well as be a worship service for everyone.

During the active dying period, we began writing Loren's obituary. All these tasks took thought and time. It is not easy to write this kind of description in a hurry or at the last minute. Working on it a little at a time over the final days was helpful. It gave time for family members to contribute, edit, and ensure that the writing was appropriate and true to who Loren was.

Anatomy Bequest Program

When we had talked with Loren about how he wanted his body deposed upon his death, our daughter Mary, a pastor, reminded us of the University of Minnesota's bequest program as one consideration. This program invites all who are interested to donate their body upon death to the university medical school for study and research. The decision can be made at any time during one's life; decisions cannot be made on behalf of another person after death.

When one decides to become a donor, an application is completed, signed by the donor, and returned to the bequest program, where it is kept on file. The research program is used primarily for the purpose of teaching anatomy to first-year medical, dental, and physical therapy students. After learning the details of the bequest program, Loren was much in favor of becoming a donor. As a family we felt that, through his donation, his teaching would continue after his death and help many. I have since also signed up to become a donor upon my death.

> *From the Journal ~*
>
> *Today we signed Dad up to be a donor of his body to the Anatomy Bequest Program at the U of M. . . . Many of their donors are educators and veterans. "These are people who want to keep giving." My dad liked this notion. As an educator to the end, and a vet,[1] being a donor is a good fit. —Mary (child #3)*

Several months after Loren's death, the University of Minnesota anatomy students sent an invitation to all families whose loved ones had donated their bodies in the past year

---

[1] Loren served in the U.S. Navy during World War II.

to attend an evening program. It was held at Northrup Auditorium on the university campus. The university anatomy students planned and hosted the program—a well-prepared program of music, readings, reflections, and slide show featuring a picture of each donor—in honor of our loved ones, "whose selfless donation serves as a fountain of wisdom for each of us." A beautiful reception followed, with students visiting and mingling with the families, expressing their gratitude and appreciation.

The Final Breath and What Followed

All five of our children, Paul, Mark, Mary, Becky, and Joel, were present when Loren drew his last breath. The last child, Paul, arrived only 15 minutes before Loren died. I was grateful they were all present at that moment. Even though Loren had not responded or been able to communicate with us during the last few days of his life, I wondered whether some consciousness still did not remain and play a part in his dying. For example, did Loren hang on to life until Paul was there? Is some hearing capability still present even when it would appear not to be so? Death is a great mystery.

> *From the Journal ~*
>
> *My beloved Loren died at 2:00 this afternoon. . . .The last words spoken to Loren by Paul were, "Mom, Paul, Mark, Mary, Becky, and Joel are all here. May you go in peace. It's okay for you to go."*

When one is in hospice care and death comes, hospice is notified first, not 9-1-1. Jean, our primary hospice nurse, had made a visit shortly before Loren died. When we called her after he had died, we discovered she was still in the apartment complex where we live. She had stopped on her way out to record notes from her visit. She returned quickly to our apartment and began attending to many of the details, including disposing of remaining narcotics and other prescription medications in a responsible way. The drugs would not be flushed down the toilet, Jean said. Instead, she crushed all the medications together and mixed them with detergent (what a terrible potion) and put it in a bag in the trash. It is important not to have narcotics, or other potentially harmful medications, kept unsecured in the home. Besides their having "street value," there is always a temptation for others to use these medications inappropriately.

Jean also notified the university bequest program. A program representative called soon to inform us that representatives would pick up Loren's body whenever we were ready but assured us his body could remain in our home for as much time as we needed. Pastor Susan, one of our pastors, was notified and stopped by that afternoon, shared prayers, and spent time with us.

After two or more hours of remembering and sharing with one another around Loren's body, we called the bequest program people and informed them we were ready to release his body. Soon, two men, dressed in suit and tie, appeared at our door, offered their condolences, and with great care and respect removed Loren's body on a gurney. At such sensitive and final moments the protocol and procedures used are critically important. It is a moment one remembers clearly. The moment had arrived. The moment I had waited for, yet, unrealistically, hoped would never come. My emotions were flat.

Celebrating Loren's Life

Despite my exhaustion and empty feelings, life had to go on. The first thing was the celebration of life service that was to be held at Gloria Dei. It overflowed with family, friends, and colleagues. Each child took part in the service in some way—Paul gave a eulogy he had written, Mary read a poem she had penned, Joel, Mark and Becky each read one of the three Scripture lessons. Becky played her flute during the prelude. Each of the seven grandchildren also had a part in the service. Anna, Peder, Leah, and Maya assisted with the distribution of Holy Communion, Siri played the piano during the communion distribution, and Jonathan and Jennifer assisted the pastors with the Remembrance of Baptism liturgy. During the singing of the first hymn, "Shall We Gather at the River," the congregation was sprinkled with water that Jonathan and Jennifer carried in large shells. Shells are a symbol of baptism and of pilgrimage and journey. The Norway pine branches used for the sprinkling came from the ARC woods.

In addition to classical music, Loren had loved choral music. A volunteer choir of many voices came from Becky and Mary's churches, and from Gloria Dei. The choir performed two selections, the beloved chorale "O Day Full of Grace," by F. M. Christiansen, and a more recent composition by Stephen Paulus, with text by Michael Dennis Browne, entitled, "Pilgrim's Hymn." The second and last verse of this lovely composition contains these words:

> Even with darkness sealing us in, We breathe Your name, and through all the days that follow so fast, we trust in You; endless Your grace, O endless Your grace, beyond all Mortal dream. Both now and for ever, and unto ages and ages. Amen.

These two beautifully rendered selections were soul inspiring. At the conclusion of the worship celebration, Mary ran up to the filled balcony and sang unaccompanied the hymn "My Life Flows On in Endless Song," with the concluding lines of the refrain, "How can I keep from singing," echoing throughout the church. This hymn was not printed in the bulletin, as Mary had been uncertain whether she would be able to sing. Her lovely, clear voice filled the sanctuary with a fitting, as well as emotional, ending. I felt an enormous outpouring of love flowing through every aspect of the service in word, song, and silence.

Following the service, a reception was held, though I was able to greet only some of the many people who came. Many individuals participated generously and willingly in a truly beautiful worship service. After the memorable celebration of life service was over, after receiving family and friends from near and far, and after the busyness subsided, then the great emptiness and the undeniable aloneness began to sink in.

From the Journal ~

Now Loren knows in full and is fully known. His questions are answered, the mystery is revealed, and all things have become new. . . . Yes, I dare to believe that he is beginning something new, something beautiful, something wonderful.

2 *Time Alone*

The day arrived when I was alone. After family members had stayed with me for several nights, following Loren's death and the celebration of life service, I assured them they did not need to stay any longer. I would be fine.

Strange as this may sound, having some time alone was welcome at first. I appreciated the quiet and the time to begin to really take in the meaningful gatherings, the messages, the cards, all the happenings of the past days and weeks. I had been surrounded by so many for so long. But life had changed drastically for me, and I had changed too. As James E. Miller wrote in *Winter Grief, Summer Grace*, "You will never again be the person you once were. You will have lost, but in addition to the losing—because of the losing—you will have gained."

From the Journal ~

I do not face the future with fear. However, I can imagine there will be days of deep loneliness and emptiness. I will try to walk through these times with trust and confidence remembering that I am really not alone.

During the months of Loren's confinement, I was at home most of the time other than to make a quick trip to the store, attend church when possible, and through the encouragement of my family try to get outdoors for a walk or outing. Grief seemed to come in waves during the first weeks and months following Loren's death. I never knew what would trigger tears: a word, a song, a gesture, a picture. Sometimes tears just came.

After everything quieted down, and after several months of seclusion, I felt hesitant to make that first foray out into public places where I was known. I wondered how I would respond to the inevitable questions and inquiries I was sure to face. My hesitation proved to be an idle concern. With every person I met, I felt their embrace, their understanding, and their loving care. Feeling so warmly welcomed and received following my absence brought encouragement to move on with life. I was beginning another journey—a journey of healing and reentry. This too, would be a process, hard work, new learning, and new growth.

Developing a New Outlook on Life Alone

During the first weeks after Loren's death, I was frequently asked, "How are you doing?" Quite honestly, I did not know how to respond. I myself did not know. I was walking in a world that at times did not seem real. I was walking a road I had never been on before. The person who had been a daily part of my life for more than 57 years was no longer present, although I felt him everywhere. In a 1931 letter to friends, Edna St. Vincent Millay wrote insightfully regarding the loss of her mother, "The presence of that absence is everywhere." The daily rituals, the established ways of doing things in small and large matters—things I had come to take for granted—were now no longer part of my day. The easy exchanges and the understanding that develops over the years between two people with just a glance or a nod were not there. This absence leaves a deep emptiness, an unexplainable void.

The attitude one develops becomes critical. How one approaches each day and with what understanding one looks at the present is essential. Will I live with regret or gratitude? Will I withdraw into myself or reach out to others? Will I be able to enjoy life again? Henri Nouwen, a Dutch writer and theologian said, "We always have a choice to live the moment as a cause for resentment or as a cause for joy." Early on I decided I wanted to live with gratitude rather than regret. I knew this was a tall order. Could I do it? Although this objective has been imperfectly lived out, it is important to have the intention and goal before me.

Rekindling Simple Awareness

To have a purpose and goal helps me be more deliberate in finding ways to be grateful: in my surroundings, in my encounters, in my walks, and in ordinary happenings. There are so many if I but pay attention. It is said that the more we look, the more we see; the more we listen, the more we hear. A simple practice, yet so true. Can my looking be so intentional that I see the extraordinary in the ordinary? Cultivating a practice of mindfulness to the gifts surrounding me can awaken the senses to see more, hear more, and feel more.

In this regard I remember a personal yet ordinary experience I had many years ago that became an extraordinary experience of mindfulness of the presence of God. I was walking in the countryside on a beautiful sunny day with no agenda other than to enjoy the day. I had a notepad and pencil in my pocket. I came to a large, beautiful tree with branches that seemed to invite me to rest in its shade. I sat down simply to enjoy the scene before me. A gentle breeze swayed the surrounding trees. Their vibrant autumn leaves shimmered in the sun. The sun's warmth penetrated my being as I watched the subtle movements of the stately trees and was delighted by the sights and sounds of my surroundings. I remembered my notepad in my pocket and decided to take it out and write down all that I saw and all that I heard. The more I looked, the more I saw—colors, designs, shapes, forms. The more I listened, the more I heard—birds chirping, leaves rustling, animal sounds, distant sounds. The list on my notepad seemed endless.

I discovered gifts surrounding me that had always been there, yet I had not taken time to look or listen or smell or touch the richness that was there. It was a reminder to me of how profoundly and intimately the simple and the natural—the ordinary—that surrounded me could touch me. I still remember this as a special moment: a discovery of the ordinary that had power to open up new vistas and bring a sense of renewal and empowerment to me because I stopped to pay attention. That day I experienced something of the truth of which Julian of Norwich[1] spoke about centuries before, "The fullness of joy is to behold God in everything."

---

[1] A fourteenth-century English mystic and recluse. At age 30, Julian experienced several intense visions of Jesus, which she wrote about in her book *Sixteen Revelations of Divine Love.*

From the Journal ~

Julian of Norwich once said, "The fullness of joy is to behold God in everything."

Rekindling mindfulness to the surrounding gifts helps foster gratitude. Do I measure life by what I do not have and by what is missing? Or can I find ways to live from the storehouse of rich memories and experiences I have and from the daily discovered gifts in the present? It is a choice each of us must make.

Grace and Gratitude

Certainly I would have enjoyed more years with Loren to realize the plans we had been making. As humans we always want more. Rather than regret the plans we did not fulfill, my goal today is to try to live with gratitude for all I have received in the history of a long relationship. That can be challenging and rewarding. An attitude of gratitude does not take away the ongoing feelings of loneliness, emptiness, or absence, but it does help transform the difficult moments and move me to a better place. Gratitude can change the tone and color of the day. Cultivating an attitude that strives to live from gratitude rather than regret can make each day a bit richer and more life giving. Gratitude is a significant and positive tool for healing. The advice given decades ago by a beloved teacher and friend at a day retreat was, "The mark of aging well is gratitude." Cultivating a spirit of gratitude is a valuable goal for anyone at any age. The memories, opportunities, experiences, and celebrations of an individual or from a shared life can never be taken away. They remain in our memories and can be brought forth again and again to bring both gratitude and joy.

From the Journal ~

I want to share a few thoughts on gratitude. This may seem absurd at this difficult time; however, we are encouraged in Scripture to give thanks in all circumstances, including the most difficult times.

Another helpful consideration in the healing process was finding meaningful ways to be of service. Volunteering one's gifts and talents for a cause one believes in and where one wants to make a difference can be both helpful to others and can bring healing to the giver. With minimal investigation we can find countless opportunities to contribute in our community, church, or the wider world. For example, we might volunteer as a classroom assistant in the local school, help with after-school remedial programs, assist with food shelf programs or Meals on Wheels. Scripture says so beautifully in Jeremiah 29:7, "Seek the welfare of the city where I have sent you . . . for in its welfare you will find your [own] welfare." Similarly an English proverb says: "The heart that gives, gathers."

Although gratitude is my aspiration, grace is my sustenance. Grace, a theological word with broad and deep meaning, is not an abstract quality but an active working principle, making itself known through daily acts of love. Blessings come not because of any merit or claim on my part but purely as gift, freely given by a loving and gracious God. Grace represents the unconditional goodness and love of God. Grace opens the heart to gratitude. Too often, I find I operate from a place of scarcity, acting as though there will not be enough. This is limiting and restricting. God's plan is based on abundance—that there is enough for everyone when we share with one another and take only what we need. I receive grace, I operate from grace, I experience grace, yet I do not understand grace in its fullness. Grace and gratitude flow to and from each other. Anne Lamott, an American author said, “I do not at all understand the mystery of grace—only that it meets us where we are but does not leave us where it found us.”

My thoughts and experiences of gratitude and grace are beautifully summed up in these words of Henri Nouwen:

> Gratitude in its deepest sense means to live life as a gift to be received gratefully. But gratitude as the gospel speaks about it embraces all of life: the good and the bad, the joyful and the painful, the holy and the not so holy. . . . Jesus calls us to recognize that gladness and sadness are never separate, that joy and sorrow really belong together, and that mourning and dancing are part of the same movement. . . . I am gradually learning that the call to gratitude asks us to say “everything is grace.”

The Power of Symbols

At the end of the first year after Loren's death, I decided to rearrange my apartment as a small gesture of creating something new. My children came to help me, and with enthusiasm, excitement, and creativity, together we moved every piece of furniture (or so it seemed) and rearranged pictures until we were satisfied with the new look. Life was beginning again for me, often in ways I did not anticipate or fully understand. I was entering something new.

> *From the Journal ~*
>
> *[Our good friend Harry Nurmet] was a professional artist, with much of his art reflecting flowers, nature, religious themes, and his beloved Estonia. . . . We have eight of Harry's paintings in our apartment.*

My desire to create something new did not suggest that the former way was inadequate or that I was trying to forget the past but rather that life was continuing to unfold and present new possibilities and opportunities. This simple gesture did help to create a spirit of newness for me. It is not the change itself that is important but rather the symbolism and meaning it provides.

Symbols are important and do matter. They honor relationship, love, and commitment. During the last weeks of Loren's life, we talked about ways we could retain a sense of connection with each other after he had died. This seemed important to him, as well as to me. What could I do that would accomplish that? Loren had not once removed the wedding band from his finger since it had been first slipped on, the day of our wedding. I suggested that upon his death, I would have the ring removed and wear it on a chain as a necklace. This idea seemed to please him very much.

When Jean, the hospice nurse, returned to our home shortly after Loren died, I asked if she could remove the ring. I had not been able to. After wearing this ring for more than 57 years, it seemed to have become part of his flesh: it was deeply imbedded in his finger. She said she could. After a few moments she returned from the bedroom, dangling the ring from her fingers.

"How did you do that?" I asked.

"It's a secret," she replied. Not willing to let the subject go, I plied her with more questions until she confessed, "It was Crisco!" I wore the ring as a necklace for several weeks, until it seemed easier and more practical to wear it on my right ring finger together with a birthstone ring of my mother's. Although Loren's wedding band is too large for my finger, wearing it behind my mother's ring prevents it from falling off.

Anniversary

One year after Loren's death, the university medical school had completed its use of Loren's body. The bequest program offers two options to the families for deposing the body after completion of their studies: cremation or returning the body for burial. Earlier Loren and I had chosen cremation, and the program notified me that Loren's cremated remains could be either picked up by the family or mailed to me. I decided to personally pick them up.

Two weeks later on a windy, cold March day, Mary, Becky, and I arranged to go to a special restaurant for a leisurely breakfast before picking up the ashes. Although it was now more than a year after Loren's death, I knew this would be an emotional moment, and it was important for me to have family with me. The bequest program is located on the university campus near the large university hospital complex. We had previously established the time we would arrive. Because only designated people are allowed in the bequest program area, we stood and waited in the large and cold lobby after we checked in. After some minutes, a representative arrived and unceremoniously handed me a small box in which a 2- to 3-quart, heavy-duty plastic bag held the ashes. The casual manner in which the ashes were given to me was a disappointment. This had been a significant moment for us. I called the bequest office a day or two later and suggested they consider having a small private room where families could wait and the ashes could be received. The suggestion was graciously received with assurance they would consider my suggestion.

After returning home, I wondered where I would keep the ashes. I discovered that the box with the ashes fit perfectly into a small Norwegian "rosemaled" (Norwegian folk painting) 1843 heirloom chest I had received from my father and that he had received from his grandmother. I placed the chest with the ashes underneath an open end table next to a chair where Loren usually sat in our living room. I wondered how it would feel to have the ashes in our home. I quickly realized that although the box did contain Loren's ashes, it did not contain his spirit. His spirit could not be confined to a box. He was with me in quite another way.

On May 22, two months later, all the children and spouses and some of the grandchildren and I buried Loren's ashes at the ARC Retreat Center. The carefully prepared ritual and service we had planned as a family became a memorable and beautiful final farewell.

Our trip from Minneapolis had been delayed that afternoon because of severe weather conditions. In fact, a tornado did touch down in North Minneapolis that afternoon, causing severe damage. After two hours of waiting out the storm, uncertain whether we would be able to go at all, we ventured out. When we finally arrived at ARC late in the afternoon, we felt especially blessed to be greeted by a beautiful, calm, clear day and a bright shining sun. The earth was freshly cleansed by the heavy rains and glistened in the bright sun. After the storm, calm; after the struggle, release; after the pain, joy—a mirror of my own emotions.

We began our little service with a silent walk through a small portion of the beautiful ARC woods so familiar to Loren. These woods contained tall, majestic white pines, together with an assortment of oaks and other trees. Loren and I had spent several months in the spring and summer of 1976 cutting down both large and small trees, grubbing out brush and the dense undergrowth in preparation for building the retreat lodge. The ARC center consists of a large cedar log lodge, a several-car garage and workshop, and an additional log cabin that contains a staff residence, as well as additional retreat space and one individual hermitage.

Two of our sons, Paul and Joel, the oldest and the youngest child, led the procession carrying the small Norwegian chest containing the ashes. Our silent walk ended at the "Ruth tree" in the backyard of the center. Many years previously, the ARC staff had planted this flowering crab tree in my honor after my retirement. The tree now had attained some stature, approximately 10 to 12 feet tall. Peeking from the branches were swollen buds of pink, ready to burst open. Our son Paul and Mark's wife, Lisa, dug a small hole in front of the tree.

Standing in a circle, the family shared a call to worship, sang hymns, and read Scripture passages, followed by each person sharing a memory of their father, father-in-law, and grandfather. Each person also participated in putting Loren's ashes into the ground. As all life returns to dust, so Loren's ashes were placed directly into the earth without a box. Although Loren had been an academic by profession, he was also a man of the earth, a fix-it man, one who loved to work with his hands. In many ways he was a farmer at heart with practical and earthy values. He believed in the importance of recycling and composting. He believed what came from the earth should be returned to the earth to regenerate and enrich the soil. The placement of Loren's ashes directly into the soil at a place he loved so much continues his participation in that ongoing cycle of regeneration and new life. Flowers brought by daughter Mary and son-in-law Dan were placed beside the small mound.

Following the simple and meaningful committal service, an evening meal was shared in the ARC dining room that looked out on the Ruth tree and small burial mound. ARC is special to us, a place where many from our family participated significantly in the original construction. Loren and I first had seen this beautiful piece of land, which later would be given to ARC, on February 6, 1976, a cold, wintry day. Now 35 years later on a gloriously sunny day, Loren had returned to his beloved ARC to complete his earthly journey.

A Suitable Marker

After the burial of Loren's ashes, I felt it important to have a marker placed at the site. What would be appropriate? I spoke with the owner of a stone-engraving firm in a Minneapolis suburb and expressed my wish for a nontraditional marker that would fit in the country setting of a retreat center. He suggested we consider a fieldstone. He had a variety of stones for sale. He encouraged us, however, to search for a stone on land that had significance for Loren and the family. He agreed to do the engraving and suggested the stone not be too large, yet large enough so it could not be easily picked up and moved.

I asked our son Joel if he would look for a stone at the cabin he and his wife, Carol, had built on Gunflint Lake in northern Minnesota. Loren had spent considerable time helping with the construction of their cabin, as well as often enjoying the beautiful northern Minnesota wilderness area.

Joel began his search but already knew, from his familiarity with the surrounding area, a particular stone he had admired and walked past many times over the years. This would be the stone, he thought.

When Joel lifted the stone to move it into his van, the stone split in two. Fortunately, the split resulted in two perfect pieces without any splintering or crumbling. The grain in the stone was beautiful, and we knew it would only be enhanced when professionally cleaned. Joel brought the stone, or rather, stones, to Minneapolis for my approval. I readily agreed with his decision—the stones were beautiful. The original search to find one stone now had unexpectedly become two stones. The symbolism of the two stones seemed to naturally represent the life Loren and I had shared. This was an unplanned yet wonderful turn of events. One stone would be a marker for Loren, and the other, a marker for me when my ashes will also one day be placed at ARC. This felt right.

I wanted the wording on the markers to be simple yet meaningful. After conferring with family, and after many attempts at appropriate wording, a decision was reached. Loren was known for his creative sayings and comments. The inscription would be one of his own oft-used phrases. Loren believed that the resources he needed were never far away. In some instances they were as close as the person nearest him, so we had engraved:

God Hides In Those Closest To Us For Strategic Reasons
Loren E. Halvorson
March 18, 1927–February 15, 2010

The inscription on the other stone, meant for my marker, was a basic theme I often used during retreats. The deeper we listen to the self and the movement of God within, the more our horizons will be widened to include the suffering world:

A Deepened Self In A Widened World
Ruth I. Halvorson
July 16, 1929–

3 *Now What?*

Following the death of our loved ones, it is comforting to hear their name spoken and hear stories about them. Some people believe that by not speaking the name of the loved ones and not sharing stories about them, they will spare the grieving from more grief.

Helping One Who Is Grieving

I recall a clergyman sharing his experience with me after the death of his wife. Both friends and family had made a concerted effort after her death not to mention her name or talk about her in his presence, thinking that hearing her name and stories about her would only add to his grief. The reality was just the opposite. More than ever, he said, he needed to hear her name again and again and anecdotes shared about her.

From the Journal ~

Today I've been thinking about this familiar Isaiah passage: "I have called you by name, you are mine. . . ." How special to be . . . remembered so personally, and welcomed so warmly.

In other instances, some are unsure as to what is appropriate to say to the grieving person at the time of death. That first moment of face-to-face contact with a person after the death of a loved one can be awkward. People may feel uncertain how to appropriately express their condolences and concern. Another friend shared an experience she had after the death of her husband. On a walk one day, she saw a friend approaching in the distance. Before they met, the friend crossed the street, uncertain how to express her sympathy and condolences face to face,.

From my experience, it is not how well expressed and articulate the condolences are but rather the intention and act itself. When words arise from the heart, they touch and communicate regardless of how well spoken they are. Many times, words are not needed. The presence of friends and family, the clasp of a hand, or a tender embrace may speak more eloquently than words. Gestures of care and concern can be expressed in a multitude of ways: cards, handwritten notes, telephone calls, brief visits, prepared meals, food items, flowers, memorial gifts, an invitation to lunch or coffee, or an invitation to go for a walk. Gestures large or small given in a spirit of love convey an important message of care and remembrance.

Following a Sunday morning worship service at my church during Loren's confinement, a friend approached me and expressed her gratitude for my CaringBridge journal entries and said, "I reach out and touch you every day." How deeply I felt her words.

To Love Again

Another important question to ask after the death of a loved one is whether it is possible to love again. When we have lost a great love, it is difficult to imagine anyone playing that role—spouse, partner, soul friend, confidant—in our life again. The loss can leave us feeling uncertain and unsure. It may seem impossible to ever share life in a meaningful way again. Even the thought of another relationship can be difficult to entertain. Sorrow and sadness always remain for the loss of a great love. However, the morning does come when we gradually begin to see more light and feel more life. Slowly we begin to emerge from the darkness when life begins to flow more naturally.

As every person is unique, so the need and desire for another relationship will vary. We are not islands unto ourselves. We all need human relationships. How we satisfy that need becomes our challenge. For some, there is no desire for another intimate relationship. For others, the longing remains strong. This may come as a surprise. The desire for another marriage relationship may be precisely because of having known a wonderful shared life. A new relationship does not minimize or diminish the prior commitment but becomes a new relationship to cultivate and enjoy. It is an opportunity to share more deeply and meaningfully again and fill a void.

Another type of relationship might mean companionship only. This may be particularly true for persons who are older and who have known a long marriage. For me, I don't desire remarriage. What I long for is a trusted companion with whom I could share conversations, walks, concerts, plays, lectures, and other events. I have friends who have lost their spouse after a long relationship and later met a person with whom they felt comfortable and compatible. This new friendship offered them opportunity to enjoy conversations, concerts, plays, and each other's company. The joy and companionship of such a relationship satisfies a need, yet marriage is not desired.

We do not create love—we receive love, love is a gift. A gift of God. God is love and the source of love. Grief is the price we pay for the loss of a deep love. Although I no longer know, in the same way, the love I knew so richly during Loren's life, yet I continue to live from that love through rich memories, through a legacy of letters, poems, and limericks, and through our children. Life has become more valuable and precious because I have walked beside death.

I want to live life fully now, and I know Loren would want that. It is up to me to participate as completely as I can in creating an ongoing, meaningful life. I have already experienced many unexpected surprises in the unfolding of this new journey. Connections have been made, invitations have come, and serendipitous encounters have happened, opening up surprising possibilities and opportunities. Yes, there are times of aching loneliness and emptiness—I expect that and must accept that, but I know now it is possible to create something new, something that can spring from the darkness of grief. Yes, new life is emerging. I remain open to the fresh winds of the spirit blowing in my life, continually birthing new possibilities and new life even in the midst of loss and grief—a great paradox.

I must trust my inner truth, God within, and listen for the promptings of my heart that emerge. My own formation has been shaped and influenced through faith practices, experience, struggle, grief, and the power of love. When we listen and wait and then act on the leading of our heart, it becomes the truest expression of the self.

> *From the Journal ~*
> *Borrowing from Julian of Norwich, we pray "in the certainty that all is well, that all shall be well, and all manner of things will be well, for all rest in You."*

One Final Message

Some time after Loren died, I was looking for something in one of my dresser drawers in our bedroom. In my search I came upon an envelope addressed "Ruthie." It was from Loren. A letter to be opened after he died. I hesitantly and nervously opened the envelope. Along with the letter, Loren had included two pages of four- and eight-line verses he had written for me to read—one verse each day for the next several weeks. These verses were written earlier when he had still been able to use the computer. For the next several moments, I was transfixed as I read:

> Sweetheart,
>
> I am not gone but present in ways that cannot be comprehended during our life on earth. Each day we will be in touch beyond the daily verses I am leaving you for the next months, but in the mystery of "presence" about which we only had faint hints before. I know you will feel lonely, but I hope that deep within, you will in truth not feel alone.
>
> Since our children contain both our genes, I hope that you will sense my presence in them as my way of being with you. And as you see the unfolding of the fruits of our shared labors in church and

society, these will also provide signs of presence. How I will be part of you I do not know as I write this, but I do know that now and take comfort in the hope of not having to leave you.

Words are not adequate to express my love for you. You are a gift of God who graced, enriched, deepened and nurtured my life for 57 years. One could not ask for more and one need not ask for more. My gratitude has grown every year and hope that my final abiding legacy is the transformation of your sadness to a deeper joy, the kind that now I am experiencing so profoundly. When Jesus said that he would be always with us, I now realize that that was a promise for us all in the community of saints on earth as in heaven. And that is the incredible goodness contained in our last "good" bye.

I love you eternally,

Loren

I remembered again that middle-of-the-night, tender, heart-to-heart talk Loren and I had had late in his confinement when he asked, "How will we stay connected?" In addition to wearing his wedding ring as I promised, the hours I have spent in writing my experiences of loss and grief, anguishing over how to honestly and helpfully write my story, has in fact revived and revitalized my connection with Loren. Through the writing, I have felt his presence, an unseen yet constant companion. This labor of love has deepened our connection and love in a mysterious way,

"Everything is grace."

Appendix A
Complete CaringBridge Journal

Tuesday, November 3, 2009

Hello friends,

As you may have heard, Loren and family recently learned that his prostate cancer (something he has lived long and well with for nearly 20 years) has spread to many places in his body—places far from the prostate. After several visits to multiple doctors and a 16-day course of radiation, it has become clear that the ill effects of treatment are not worth the possible benefit. On Friday, October 30, a hospice team entered our world. Loren is at home at Becketwood,[1] attended by family and the hospice team. The change in his health has been fast. We are all on a fast learning curve of how to best take care of Loren, each other, and ourselves. We don't have it figured out yet, and your prayers will help!

---

[1] An independent living senior cooperative in Minneapolis

We have set up this CaringBridge site so that you might keep tabs on how Loren and Ruth are doing and so that you can send messages in the guestbook. Be assured that all messages sent will be read and appreciated. For the time being, this mode of communication is better than phone, since the "rest times" at home are important—and unpredictable! Thank you for your consideration and your prayers.

~ *Lisa (daughter-in-law, wife of Mark)*[2]

Thursday, November 5, 2009

Your messages on the CaringBridge website are a source of great encouragement and hope in the midst of the darkness of these days. Early in my life, I was dramatically introduced to the powerful truth that there is "grace at point zero," a phrase German friends used to describe the "surprise" that out of the horror of World War II, new life emerged in church and society. And now it is my joyful discovery that in my own dark night, I am experiencing grace at point zero, which comes each day in the affirmation of friends and family. In what you have shared is evidence that the seeds that Ruth and I have sown are bearing fruit, despite so much turmoil in our personal and public lives.

Here are some of the signs that bring hope for me: connecting the heart and the head. The seminary where I taught for many years has invited a Canadian Lutheran, who was for 19 years a monk at Taizé[3], to teach courses

---

[2] Unless otherwise noted, all entries are by Ruth Halvorson.

[3] An ecumenical monastic men's community in France

in worship and confessions. This promises a partnership between the training of clergy and the ministry of ARC,[4] which was Ruth's dream from the beginning.

Since I worked for many years with the colleges on vocation, the news brought just the other day by a friend—that one of our colleges is launching a visionary program for a doctor's degree in nursing drawing from the riches of holistic health care in this country and Africa and the Native American communities—is very good news to me.

I was moved just today by a lead editorial in our daily paper of how the recent decision of our national church[5] is a sign of grace to many who have been excluded. The words of the writer were especially profound to me, that the church's vote removes the fear and terror of a God bent on making "one whole category of people eternally anxious about their salvation."

Your expressions of personal love and concern make me feel that I am moving closer and closer to life, not death. And for this I am deeply grateful.

With love and affection,
~ *Loren*

Thursday, November 5, 2009

We are tremendously encouraged and uplifted by your CaringBridge entries. Each and every entry makes an important connection for us with you.

---

[4] "Action, Reflection, Celebration"; an ecumenical retreat center

[5] The ELCA's decision to allow congregations to call and ordain gays and lesbians in committed monogamous relationships to serve as clergy

We started on the hospice program last Friday and are realizing all the benefits of this wonderful program. Yesterday Loren had a music therapist here singing and playing on her gentle instrument she carried with her. We have had nurse visits, social worker visits, and doctor visits, and tomorrow a home health aide comes.

In addition to the hospice workers, we have had a constant presence here with someone from our wonderful family. We are traveling in new territory and are learning every day how to best care for Loren and for one another.

Please know that we are grateful for your greetings, your concerns, and your prayers. It is good to know that at times when it seems difficult to pray, we are being held in prayer by all of you.

Saturday, November 7, 2009

Today is a warm, glorious fall day! Lisa took Loren out in the wheelchair, traveling on the newly surfaced Parkway walking paths along the Mississippi River in Minneapolis, so it was a smooth ride. This outing was very much enjoyed by Loren, but at the same time also tiring. He has some very good moments when he especially enjoys short visits with friends and family. He has also had some dark moments that we as family seek to understand.

Last evening we had a wonderful gathering of all our children.[6] It was a special time for Loren to share as well as for each family member to share.

---

[6] Son Paul, son Mark and spouse, Lisa, daughter Mary and spouse, Dan, daughter Becky and spouse, Dan, and son Joel and spouse, Carol.

Again, please know how very much your messages mean to us.

Monday, November 9, 2009

I have entered messages on CaringBridge before for others, but I had not fully realized the impact and encouragement it can be for the ones who are recipients of these messages. Thank you, thank you! I read and reread your messages to Loren.

Over the weekend Loren had wonderful visits with his grandson, Peder, a student at Saint Olaf;[7] his granddaughter, Anna, a new elementary school teacher; his three-year-old great-granddaughter Lucy, who always brings joy to us; and his nephew, David, from Briarcliff, New York. And of course throughout the day someone from our immediate family was always here. We feel so loved and supported.

Although it was a beautiful day yesterday, Loren did not have the desire or the interest to venture outside. Today we will try again.

Last night Loren had one of his best nights—he slept through most of the night. We feel blessed and grateful for the many intimate and meaningful moments we have had throughout these days. We feel surrounded with love.

---

[7] Lutheran college in Northfield, Minnesota

Tuesday, November 10, 2009

Paul, our oldest son, arrived home yesterday after having been out of town for 9 days. He lives in Minneapolis and now is also added to the around-the-clock family care schedule. In addition, we see someone from hospice care almost every day. Today Loren will have his second visit from the music therapist, whom, incidentally, we have both known for decades. It is a healing time to have such gentle, beautiful music wafting through the room. We also expect the home health aide will come today. She gives him wonderful refreshment and healing through her "royal bath."[8]

Yesterday Loren also had a most meaningful visit from Fred, a friend from Lanesboro, Minnesota. Later in the day our precious 7-month-old great-grandchild, Illiana, came with her grandpa, Joel, and brightened up our space with her winning smile.

As Loren has put it, we have had a "rich diet" these days with short, meaningful visits, intimate conversations, and incredible discoveries on this journey to life. Although there are difficult moments, we feel so blessed to have these intentional days to connect at remarkably deep levels.

Wednesday, November 11, 2009

This evening Loren, sons Paul and Joel, daughter-in-law Carol, and new great granddaughter Illiana are gathered. Loren is eating some chicken and rice dinner, while

[8] A designation the family gave to describe her comfort-filled care

great-uncle Paul is entertaining Illiana, who is showing "GG" how she can precrawl "scoot" across the floor.

Last night Loren's older sister Betty spent the evening and better part of the day in service to her brother and was joined by younger sister Gayle (visiting from Norway).[9] Meanwhile today, Ruth visited the doctor. Concerned by her high blood pressure, daughter-in-law Lisa encouraged Ruth to visit Saint Joseph's hospital in Saint Paul. Ruth was joined at the hospital by daughters Becky and Mary. Ruth had a slew of tests, which all came back negative. However, her doctor encouraged her to spend one night in the hospital for observation. We are grateful for all the love and support. Keep the messages coming; they are greatly enjoyed by Loren, Ruth, and family.

~ *Joel (child #5)*

Thursday, November 12, 2009

Today Loren and Ruth (via phone from her hospital bed) enjoyed a home concert given by Brenda and David, two friends who are violinists with the Saint Paul Chamber Orchestra. Ruth continues to rest at the hospital for a second day and is planning an R & R getaway to a family condo on Lake Superior[10] with her two daughters, Becky and Mary, as soon as the doctor gives the okay for her to leave the hospital (perhaps on Friday).

This evening Loren enjoyed sharing stories with his two sisters, Betty and Gayle. During this time, we five

---

[9] Where she has lived with her family for 37 years

[10] Our son Mark and his wife, Lisa, own a condo on the North Shore of Lake Superior just outside Beaver Bay, Minnesota.

siblings with several of our spouses met to discuss a coordinated care plan for our parents.

We are grateful for the many offers of support and ask that these requests be coordinated via Loren and Ruth's daughter Becky. We are learning to provide a balance between providing care and support with time for our parents to spend together on their own.

~ *Paul (child #1)*

Saturday, November 14, 2009

A report from the North Shore:

Mom was discharged from the hospital this morning. Her final MRI, MRA, and EEG[11] were normal. We are grateful for that. She is feeling better. Before heading to the North Shore, Mom had a good visit with Dad. His comment to me was, "This is going to be my best trip to Splashing Rock,"[12] (the name of the condo where we are staying). "It is the right thing for you to do." Dad told Mom to be sure to communicate that he is very much at peace. He is moving away from his head and deeper to his heart. He also wanted to convey again how deeply meaningful it is to receive your CaringBridge messages.

We arrived at Splashing Rock about 3:00 p.m. Mom took a hot shower and was finally able to wash her hair. She came out to a waiting cup of hot tea with Mary and me to sit in front of the picture window looking out on Lake

---

[11] MRI: magnetic resonance imaging; MRA: magnetic resonance angiogram; EEG: electroencephalogram

[12] On Lake Superior

Superior. At that moment, right before us was a full blazing rainbow. We knew then, this was the right place to be. Mom said, "I know all will be well."

Back in Minneapolis Dad is being cared for by a gentle man named Francis while we are away. The rest of the family is providing care during the night shift and visiting during the day. Francis is a home health aide hired from an agency recommended by Fairview Hospice.[13] When we return home, there will be a home health aide with Mom and Dad during the day, with the family providing care for the evening and overnight. This will allow the rest of the family to be more present to Dad and Mom.

I too want to add how much it means to me to hear the outpouring of love and care for my parents. It is truly a gift during this time.

~ *Becky (child #4)*

Saturday, November 14, 2009

A couple days ago I had a very "luminous" conversation with Dad. I can honestly say that he appears serene, content, and at peace. He said that the unknown is now known, and it's been known all along, but now he is not a stranger to it. He is retelling his stories because he now has a different vantage point from which to share them. He is sifting through these experiences for the rich ingredients he may have overlooked. Life is becoming richer, more valuable, and the anxiety is gone. He does

[13] Fairview Home Care and Hospice, which serves Minneapolis and fifteen surrounding counties

not have fear. He is moving into a place of healing. This journey into death means moving even more deeply into life. Life is now more tangible and real. The mystery is becoming familiar. Time is moving more slowly; it is weighted with joy and deep meaning. There is no need to rush, to go someplace else. Eternity is now. Heaven and earth are intertwined. We agreed that perhaps eternity is "the fullness of time."

These kinds of holy conversations are the gift Dad is giving to those who sit with him as he holds their hand. He continues to teach; he is doing his own research now. The intellect has been gently led deep to the heart.

~ *Mary (child #3)*

Saturday, November 14, 2009

Report from Loren's bedside.

While holding my dad's hand, he shared with me: "I'm not waiting for heaven; I'm experiencing it right now. The amazing thing is that it isn't something new, but something old and familiar and very warm." He expressed his gratitude for everyone's heartfelt greetings and shared that all of your expressions of love are helping him experience heaven now.

In gratitude,

~ *Mark (child #2)*

Sunday, November 15, 2009

Tonight, Dad declared that he is ready to let go and has made his peace with dying. This was shared in a tender moment with his son and daughter-in-law.[14] Though we know not the time, he is prepared and living in a state of grace and gratitude.

These are special days of making amends, of forgiving and being forgiven, of sharing and expressing love between friends and family. Our time these days is spent in listening, expressing love, holding hands, providing support and comfort, and being a gentle presence. In a small way, as children, we are giving back to the one who originally helped to give us life. The cycle of life continues for all of us. We are eternally grateful.

~ *Paul (child #1)*

Sunday, November 15, 2009

I have spoken with Loren several times today from the North Shore condo where I am spending a few days with daughters, Mary and Becky. This time away was strongly suggested by our family, and the beautiful serene quietness here is proving to be most healing and renewing. When speaking with Loren this morning, I said I was sorry that I have not been with him the past several days. "You are in the right place. This will be the best trip I have ever made to the North Shore. I will be living each moment with you." He assured me that "intimacy is not based on proximity." He mentioned that life is moving more slowly and on its own and does not require a lot now. He is most certainly savoring each visit, every kindness and gesture, and every CaringBridge message.

---

[14] Mark and his spouse, Lisa

I remain grateful for renewing health, for the generous outpouring of love and care, and for the deep peace and calmness Loren is experiencing.

Sunday, November 15, 2009

From the North Shore of Lake Superior.

Today was also a significant day in Minneapolis. Several months ago I asked Dad to preach at University Lutheran Church of Hope,[15] the congregation where my family are currently members and where Dad was baptized, confirmed, and ordained. When it became clear that Dad was unable to deliver the sermon due to his failing health, he asked me to deliver his sermon. With Mom's recent hospitalization, and Mary and I deciding to accompany Mom to the North Shore for a continued time of rest, Dad decided to have my husband, Dan, preach. Dad thought having Dan, who grew up Catholic, would add a wonderful ecumenical touch. Dan preached Dad's sermon "Is the End the Beginning?"[16] at both services today. People were very touched by the sermon, especially the ending poem "God Spoke to Me," which Dad wrote on 9/28/09:

God spoke to me the other day,
A woman's voice, God's not just a "he"
It was a surprising experience,
Sounded just like my wife, Ruthie.

---

[15] ELCA congregation located in Minneapolis

[16] See appendix B for full sermon.

Later God said "I love you"
This time in a masculine voice
I'd swear was our oldest son,
It seems that God can make that choice.
God kissed me the other day,
Right on the lips intimately;
And you know what it really felt like?
Like my great-granddaughter Lucy.
God did promise to live right here in us,
Which is not very far away;
You know the neat thing about that?
It's you can be with God every day.
"Got some time next week?" I asked.
It's fun talking with the deity.
"Got all the time in the world" said God.
"How about an eternity?"

~ Becky (child #4)

Monday, November 16, 2009

Today Mary, Mom and I returned from the North Shore, arriving home early afternoon. Dad was resting when we arrived. He spent the morning visiting with his two sisters and had a goodbye conversation with Gayle, who flies back to Norway tomorrow. Dad told me that it took a lot out of him to say his goodbye.

Dad seems to tire more easily—though in the midst of his tiredness, he has a sense of humor. When I told him I would be spending the night in the bed next to him, he said, "I suppose you're getting used to sleeping with preachers." The last couple nights, I shared a bed on the North Shore with my sister Mary, an ELCA pastor.

I have taken a two week family medical leave to help coordinate care on the home front. In talking with Mom and reading Dad's energy level, we feel at this time it's best to limit visits, as any activity takes a lot of energy. The CaringBridge site has been a gift to help share memories, thoughts, and concerns, and he looks forward to hearing these read to him throughout the day. At this point Dad is wanting to spend time with family and especially with Mom.

~ *Becky (child #4)*

Tuesday, November 17, 2009

Loren had a very good rest last night, sleeping from 10 p.m. until 5:30 a.m. This was indeed good, as the day was filled with poignant and meaningful visits and talks with family about end of life. These closure conversations are giving him much peace. One of these conversations was with brother in-law Ruben, from Rock Island, Illinois, who paid us a visit this morning. Loren also made a follow-up call with Ruben's wife, Thelma, who is Ruth's sister. Ruben's comment to Becky and me after his visit with Loren was, "Fantastic! He is gracious to the end."

Together with visits from the immediate family, visits from the hospice nurse, massage therapist, hospice volunteer, seminary friend, it was a very full day. These conversations are very important to Loren. Loren said, "There's a place in the Bible that says we will be given the word at the right time. I believe I've been given the words as I need them. I'm not planning what I'm going to say anymore, but during these closure conversations the words are there. Wow . . . Wow!" We believe Loren is talking more from the heart these days than from his head. He would say so himself.

We thank you again for your CaringBridge messages. We look forward to reading them each day.

Tuesday, November 17, 2009

I want to share two sweet and touching stories that also have a bit of humor in them. When Mom told Dad, "I'm going to miss you so much. Half of me will be gone when you are not here. Our lives have been so intertwined and interconnected," Dad's response was, "I'm going to talk to those technicians in heaven and have them set up a system so I can keep in touch with you." The other story was concerning whether he would recognize his loved ones in heaven. Dad said, "If I can't recognize Ruthie in heaven, I ain't going there."

These days are filled with emotional connections, times of laughter, and feeling grateful for being together in such a significant way.

~ *Becky (child #4)*

Wednesday, November 18, 2009

This was again a very full day for Loren. His wish is to have a final closure conversation with each member of our family. These conversations began yesterday, continued today, and will continue for the next several days. Each of these conversations has been very personal, heartfelt, poignant, and beautiful but also emotionally and physically draining for him. Loren continues to say that he does not plan what he is going to say in advance but trusts the moment, and the right words come. I believe that these conversations may be his finest teaching—teaching that comes directly from the heart. I feel he has honed everything down to the essentials, to what is real, lasting, and gives life. Gratitude is on his lips and on mine for the incredible life that we have shared together, for the opportunities we have had, for the encounters and experiences we have known, and for the rich faith in which we have grown together over the years.

One of the family conversations today was with granddaughter, Maya, who shares a birthday (March 18) with Loren. Today on the eighteenth of November, they celebrated their "two-thirds birthday" with a bowl of chocolate ice cream. Maya, who will be 12 on her next birthday, said she will light an extra candle on her cake for Grampa every year.

Loren is slowing down, eating less, and sleeping more. We are trying to limit his activity to primarily family.

Please know how very much your CaringBridge messages mean to all of us.

Thursday, November 19, 2009

Dad celebrated communion this afternoon with his pastor, Susan.[17] He said to her: "Today I received a

[17] From Gloria Dei Lutheran Church (ELCA) in Saint Paul

wonderful gift from Jean, [the hospice nurse]. She said, 'It's okay to go.' I am free to go whenever I want." Afterward, Jean shared with the family that "he's in a really divine place."

Then Dad requested that the entire family visit with him one on one. In all, he had sixteen conversations—with Mom, his five children and their spouses, six of seven grandchildren (the seventh, Peder made a trip from Saint Olaf College on Tuesday to see his grandpa.) Granddaughter Siri, in Norway,[18] spoke with grandpa today via Skype. At the end of this full day, the family gathered around his bed and sang hymns, ending with "Silent Night."

Dad is in a wonderful lucid place at the moment and continues to let go. It feels like the end is imminent, as Dad is now embracing two worlds with lots of peace and gratitude.

~ Paul (child #1)

Friday, November 20, 2009

After a very full day of goodbyes, kisses, and lingering hand-holding, Dad slept a good 10 hours. Today he is clearly retreating into an interior place. His family members come and hold hands, providing a vigil presence. This morning I read him the poem "Little Lamb," by William Blake. After he let the simple, childlike words sink in, he said, "Mary, I have a job for you. Collect all the theological books you can and

---

[18] Spending a year in a Folks School as a break from college

condense their material into poetry." "I'm on it, Dad," I dutifully replied.

In the midst of this thin place, Dad is full of humor and profound reflection. He smiles whimsically; he teases. He is also very quiet, no longer getting out of bed or eating. The final journey is at full throttle.

Today we signed Dad up to be a donor of his body to the Anatomy Bequest Program at the U of M.[19] He was very pleased to choose this option. His own father was on the science faculty at the U of M. All this feels like a full circle. Grace, the church I serve, is just down the street.[20] It is a familiar landscape and comforting because of this. The young man who works at the Anatomy Bequest Program received our forms and said many of their donors are educators and veterans. "These are people who want to keep giving." My dad liked this notion. As an educator to the end, and a vet,[21] being a donor is a good fit.

As the circle of gathering becomes smaller, limited to family, we are touched and comforted daily by the kindness of your words, and the compassion they portray.

Dad said this morning, "It is all blending together; I can't tell one from the other. It is beautiful. It is unreal."

---

[19] The purpose of this program, sponsored by the University of Minnesota, is to support quality education for future health professionals in the medical school and continued advancements in medical care through research.

[20] Grace University Lutheran Church, is located a block away from the university.

[21] Loren served in the U.S. Navy during World War II.

The journey to death is hard and full of its raw edges; it is also a gift when it can be shared with such gratitude, grit, and good humor. That's our dad.

~ *Mary (child #3)*

Saturday, November 21, 2009

In the early-morning hours of today, Loren and I had some precious and tender moments together declaring that there was no unfinished business between us; everything has been said—it is complete. Daughter Mary joined Loren and me and read a psalm,[22] sang a song, and said some reassuring words, and we both sang this blessing, which is sung at ARC when guests leave: "May the longtime sun shine upon you, all love surround you, and the pure light within you, guide you on your way home."

Sunday, November 22, 2009

Today Dad had another full day. In the morning I had a chance to share reflections from a moving four-day gathering just completed yesterday, titled: *Native Peoples Native Homelands Climate Change Workshop: An Indigenous Response to the Challenge.*[23]

---

[22] From a book of the Bible

[23] More information at www.nativepeoplesnativehomelands.org

This gathering of tribal, government, and academic leaders from across the country[24] culminated in an indigenous declaration that will be delivered by the White House climate negotiation teams to the UN meetings in Copenhagen next month.[25] It was an honor to participate in this gathering, and it was humbling and touching to receive prayers for Dad and the family from spiritual leaders.

Yesterday my friend and colleague Jim Rock (Sisseton-Wahpeton Dakota Nation) presented me with some braided South Dakota sweet grass to be shared with Dad. As a sacred plant to the Dakota Nation, it is used in peace and healing rituals. We burned some of the grass, and I read the draft declaration to Dad, and we listened to the closing prayer and drum ceremony, which I had been able to record.

This afternoon in between rests, Dad had a series of visits and calls. Grandchildren Leah, Maya, Jonathan, and Jennifer, and great-granddaughter Illiana visited. Arvid and Anne Bidne visited with Dad, his sister Gayle called from Norway, and the Rockwolds[26] delivered custard, which he loves. This evening Dad made a special request that each of his children visit each day. Since we all live in Minneapolis or Saint Paul, we are blessed to have the ability to easily honor this request.

---

[24] Held at the Mystic Lake Casino Hotel in Prior Lake, Minnesota, on the homelands of the Shakopee Mdewakanton Sioux Community

[25] World leaders met for climate change talks.

[26] Mary and Gaylan Rockwold, friends of the family

Dad continues to be moved by the messages left on this site. A wonderful part of his daily routine centers around listening intently to the reading of each new entry. Thanks to all for the continued prayers and support,

~ *Joel (child #5)*

Monday, November 23, 2009

Loren and I both had a very restful night. This morning we read poetry and devotions by Herb Brokering[27] that we found on his CaringBridge site. After the readings, Loren said "These are words of life from a dear friend who preceded me. How magnificent!"

After having a couple days of being mostly in bed and drinking only fluids, Loren has rebounded with new strength and energy. He got out of bed, used his walker to walk to the bathroom and living room. With this new energy also comes the difficulty of being emotionally ready and prepared to die, yet having a body that continues to have some strength. As the hospice nurse told us, it can be a hard place to be. We have no control of when death will come. Our emotions have gone up and down—shifting from what felt more imminent to believing now that we may have him with us longer than we thought. Loren is awaiting the arrival of granddaughter Siri from Norway, who arrives late tonight. Siri promises a musical concert tomorrow together with her significant friend, Brent, a very talented tenor.

---

[27] A prominent colleague, friend, churchman, and creative writer of the ELCA

Through hospice we received a recliner/lift chair that allows Loren to be in the living room, where he can be a part of the activities when he wants and feel less isolated or alone.

He so enjoys the messages you send this way. Thank you, thank you.

Tuesday, November 24, 2009

Loren sat up in his newly acquired recliner/lift chair the entire day. He slept off and on, and when awake watched the family comings and goings, which seemed to please him. He has enjoyed the ambience of the living room and the comfort of his magnificent chair.

Granddaughter Siri and friend Brent came this morning. The family circle is now complete. He has spoken personally with each child, spouse, and grandchild. Both Siri and Brent are musicians. Siri played[28] and they both sang. They will be back to share more music with Grandpa.

Loren was very quiet and reflective today. Tonight he talked about his dying and the understanding and belief we have both come to in later years that Christ's love is larger and more inclusive and expansive than we can ever imagine . . . and that is comforting.

Thank you for the many, many kindnesses that have come to us during these weeks of Loren's illness. We feel surrounded by a wonderful community here at

---

[28] Siri plays the piano beautifully.

Becketwood, as well as our church community and our community of friends and family near and far.

Wednesday, November 25, 2009

Loren had a long, good sleep last night and rested much of the morning as well in his special recliner chair. By afternoon he was alert, animated, and much like his old self. The hospice nurse, Jean, visited this morning and, among other things, discussed some of the signs of dying with Loren. However, she quickly added that each person is unique and different, and therefore everyone's dying is unique. When asked by the hospice nurse if Loren was fearful of dying, he said, "No." "Are you at peace?" Jean asked. "Oh, yes," Loren replied. "You hospice people have a wonderful ministry. I've had good counsel all along the way. I have been flooded with overwhelming signs of how this will be a wonderful experience. The richest days of my life have been given to me. I thank God for this gift. I've been gifted all my life."

At this point we feel we may have Loren with us longer than we thought at one point. Therefore, we are savoring every day and making these days as rich as possible. We began reading the book *True Compass*, by Edward Kennedy, to him this afternoon. He enjoyed that immensely, as did all of us who were here. It is a book about courage, hope, and faith.

The entire family will gather here at Becketwood tomorrow to celebrate Thanksgiving. As Henri Nouwen[29] says:

---

[29] A Dutch Roman Catholic priest, writer, and thinker of the mid-twentieth century

> Gratitude in its deepest sense means to live life as a gift to be received gratefully. But gratitude as the gospel speaks about it embraces all of life: the good and the bad, the joyful and the painful, the holy and the not so holy. . . . Jesus calls us to recognize that gladness and sadness are never separate, that joy and sorrow really belong together, and that mourning and dancing are part of the same movement. . . . I am gradually learning that the call to gratitude asks us to say "everything is grace."

Thursday, November 26, 2009

This has been a full and, in some ways, challenging day. All the children, spouses, grandchildren and friends of grandchildren, and two great-grandchildren were present today. They did not all come to our apartment. A special room here at Becketwood, called Kensington Square, located underneath the chapel, was reserved for the twenty-two of us. Loren did not venture out; however, the entire family group gathered in the turnaround in front of Becketwood before the big dinner, and Loren and I stood in the window of our apartment. We opened our third-floor windows so we could hear them all sing their table grace, which wafted up to us through the open windows, as well as their shouted greetings.

I enjoyed the meal tremendously; however, Loren could tolerate only a few bites of Jell-O and a couple bites of pie. He was not feeling up to having everyone in our apartment at one time, even for singing. Two to three family members came up at a time and briefly greeted and spoke with him. The computer-savvy family member[30] even set up Skype communication between Kensington Square and our apartment; however that proved more than Loren wanted at the time, as well. Energy levels wax and wane, as well as desire and ability to communicate with others.

I cannot minimize or begin to understand the many thoughts that must flood through one's mind and memory regarding past holidays when it was vibrant and so different. As the hospice nurse said, "Dying is hard work." Loren and I have received extravagant support and outpouring of love from our family as well as from many friends and extended family, through the good days as well as the more challenging days. We end this day, thankful for abundant blessings.

Friday, November 27, 2009

Well, it's been a quiet week in Lake Wobegon,[31] and a quiet day at Ruth and Loren's. Loren has reached a plateau in his physical health, with little ups and downs, but not big ones. Ruth has regained her strength and energy after her own hospitalization. So, after weeks of turmoil, a new routine is taking shape, and days are once again developing a rhythm. The constant presence of family members is no longer needed, though we are always at the ready! A challenge for Loren now is how to live with limited energy. This is not his usual M.O.!

---

[30] Joel

[31] Fictional town in the state of Minnesota, said to have been the boyhood home of radio humorist Garrison Keillor

Your stories, poems, and greetings on CaringBridge are a highlight of the day. Thank you, and God bless,

~ *Lisa (daughter-in-law)*

Saturday, November 28, 2009

Today was mostly a quiet day. Loren is sleeping better and sleeping more, it seems. His appetite is waning, with liquids and occasionally some soft foods being his principal diet.

Later in the afternoon, he wanted to get out of his chair and go on a little "pilgrimage." He said he had been experiencing some bleakness and told me that he didn't want bleakness to trump beauty. He began thinking of his good friend, Harry,[32] who turned 100 years old this past April and whom Loren, as a young refugee worker in Germany[33] in the late 1940s and early 1950s, had helped, along with Harry's family, to immigrate to the United State. Harry was a professional artist, with much of his art reflecting flowers, nature, religious themes, and his beloved Estonia. Harry and his wife, Linda, are also godparents to Paul, our eldest son.

We have eight of Harry's paintings in our apartment. Loren wanted to make a pilgrimage to each of these paintings and say a blessing and or prayer at each painting. This we did, moving very slowly. We remembered the blessing, beauty, and richness Harry

---

[32] Harry Nurmet, a refugee from Estonia after World War II

[33] Loren worked for the Lutheran World Federation to resettle refugees in Europe after World War II. He worked primarily with Baltic refugees and had helped Harry and his family immigrate to the United States.

has brought to us and to so many through his gift of art. We agreed that even within our own apartment, we could change bleakness into beauty by becoming more mindful and aware of what lies close at hand. Our pilgrimage today was not measured in miles but in the extraordinary beauty surrounding us. It was a sacred time.

Sunday, November 29, 2009

I was happy to be able to attend worship this morning[34] with daughter-in-law Lisa. The good word for me today was, "Advent is the anticipation of a world made whole."[35] We were encouraged to stand up and be people of audacious hope, especially in these difficult times of war, poverty, unemployment, economic challenges, health reform challenges, and more. We have the promise that God is always with us and nothing can separate us from God's love. Loren and I have certainly felt that surround of love and care.

Loren ventured out in his wheelchair to friends who live only a few doors down the hall from us for an Advent brunch. He visited briefly with the gathered guests and then returned to our apartment. This brief encounter brightened his day, as did short visits from other friends.

Our beloved children and their spouses have accompanied us every step of this journey, supporting, caring, and being very present to Loren and me. How grateful we are.

---

[34] Gloria Dei, Saint Paul

[35] In the Christian tradition, Advent is the beginning of the church year and lasts four weeks until Christmas Eve.

Monday, November 30, 2009

In some tender and reflective moments with Loren today, I realized that the dying process seems to bring extra sensitivity to one's seeing, hearing, and feeling. The dying seem to see beyond the superficial, beyond the nonessentials. Those facing death listen more carefully to what feeds their soul, what warms their heart, and the touch of a loved one's hand or a gentle kiss brings such joy and comfort. It is fundamental, basic—it's about relationship with one's loved ones, both family and friends, and with God. All else becomes unimportant.

What a journey this is!

Tuesday, December 1, 2009

Today was a good day for Loren. He had a restful night's sleep, ate better than usual, and walked around the apartment several times, although he is weaker. He also had a wonderful, soothing massage from hospice this afternoon, during which time he fell asleep. He awoke to a visit from a decades-long friend, which was a wonderful surprise and which was nurturing and much appreciated. He also connected briefly with another longtime friend via telephone. The history, the many connections, the memories of long-held relationships brings much joy and meaning to both Loren and me. Through the gift of this CaringBridge site Loren and I have felt reconnected to so many of you. Thank you. It is a gift.

Wednesday, December 2, 2009

With the help of son-in-law Dan, Loren was able to get outdoors in his wheelchair (bundled up in blankets and afghans, cap and mittens) for a short walk on the River Road. It was cold, which shortened the time outdoors; however, he was grateful for the brief encounter with the beautiful nature surrounding us here at Becketwood.

Loren definitely appears weaker and says himself that he feels weaker. After the walk and visits with people he met along the way, he rested; it was a quiet afternoon.

Every person is unique; therefore, every dying process is unique. We cannot hasten the hour nor prolong the hour. The timing rests in God's hands. In the quiet, late afternoon, we had an intimate and wonderful "heart talk." I assured him again that everything between us and between the children and grandchildren is complete. I have been told in a thousand different ways how much he loves me, and each of the children and grandchildren have, as well. We have each, in turn, expressed our deep love for him. The veil is very thin between wanting to stay and wanting to leave, between joy and sorrow, between holding on and letting go. It is a great mystery! We are savoring each moment, however long, and grateful for the insights, learnings, and love we have experienced.

Thursday, December 3, 2009

We travel more slowly these days. Each trip to the bathroom or the living room is done with greater intentionality since every step takes more strength and energy. We are grateful that Loren can still get out of bed and can move with his walker. Someone is always close at hand. His recliner/lift chair in the living room serves as both chair and bed and is where he spends the better part of each day. Perhaps the slower pace we now travel is the appropriate speed that helps us to focus on and be more aware of the moments we have. We are grateful for the times of deep joy and intimate sharing; however, there are also times when more troublesome and heavy thoughts tend to creep in. At these times, we claim the unconditional and extravagant love of God into which we can sink, feel God's forgiveness and gentle embrace.

In this Advent time, we want to wait with hope and not fear. Waiting in hope is not necessarily having our wishes fulfilled but trusting that something will be fulfilled in us in good time. I think Mary, the mother of Jesus, lived with that kind of hope and trust.

Friday, December 4, 2009

During parts of this day it appeared Loren was traveling in two worlds. I think there is a sensitivity of seeing and hearing that goes beyond what we can know or fully understand. Clearly it is a journey—the process and planning of moving from one place to another. It is indeed a great mystery that we are participating in and from which we are learning so much.

Today Loren had a bath and lotion rub-down from his wonderful home health aide and also a helpful visit from the hospice nurse. The expertise, compassion, and care we have received from hospice have been another gift to us. It is good to know that we can call them[36] at any time during the day or night if we have any concerns or problems, and they calmly provide counsel and will make an unscheduled visit too, if necessary.

Years ago I read a quote from Meister Eckhart,[37] that has stayed with me ever since: "God is not found in the soul by adding anything, but by a process of subtraction."

This is becoming a reality for Loren, I believe. He is little by little eliminating, shutting down, subtracting those things that are not necessary for the final journey. He is concerned, however, that we "keep the fires lit" for the many justice issues about which he cares so much.

Again, my deep gratitude for your CaringBridge entries, your cards, and the many kindnesses shown in countless ways.

Saturday, December 5, 2009

One of our family members stays here with us every night and is on call during the day, should I need assistance. Other members of the family drop by frequently and keep close touch via telephone. We are very fortunate to have all our children and most of our grandchildren living here in the Twin Cities.

We have listened to Advent/Christmas music today and also had more poignant, heart-to-heart conversations.

---

[36] The hospice professionals

[37] A thirteenth-century German theologian, philosopher, and mystic

The ups and downs that occur in regular, everyday life continue to occur in the days of dying, as well. Vestiges of doubt and fear tend to creep in unbidden from time to time. With deliberate honesty and forthrightness, we try to talk and pray through these concerns, or fears. I ran across this helpful quote in some of my materials the other day, "Be prepared at all times for the gifts of God and be ready always for new ones. For God is a thousand times more ready to give than we are to receive."

We have again and again been blessed with God's gifts of assurance, forgiveness, and hope.

Sunday, December 6, 2009

As we move into the heart of Advent, preparing and making ready to receive the Christ Child into our own hearts and lives, so Loren is moving inexorably into the mystery of dying, into that place unknown, yet becoming more familiar, it seems.

We have seen remarkable changes in Loren in the past 20 hours. He is sleeping much more and is considerably weaker and more detached and having moments of confusion and anxiety, as well as calmness, but clearly he is looking beyond what we are seeing. We are seeking to accompany him as gently and as lovingly and as far as we can in this journey.

Monday, December 7, 2009

As we learned from the hospice nurse today, Loren is in the active dying period. He is seeing a different reality. We have learned to validate what he says and not reorient him. At times today very poignant words were spoken by Loren, and at other times he spoke from another reality that we did not know but could only affirm. One of these special moments happened a couple days ago for me. He said, "Have I told you that I love you today?"

I said, "No, but you have told me a thousand times before that you love me."

"But have I told you a thousand times today that I love you?"

"No," I said, "not today."

"I love you, Ruthie!"

During another poignant moment today, he said, "I have taken my first step."

I asked, "How was that for you?"

"It was wonderful."

Our entire family feels so blessed and fortunate to have had this special, personal time with him and with one another. I pray that his leave-taking may be gentle and peaceful.

Tuesday, December 8, 2009

The veil between death and life is very thin. Loren is moving closer and closer in his journey home. He is not communicating much and detaching more and more. Loren was visited by our pastor, and in the late afternoon, all the children, spouses, four of the seven grandchildren, and the two great-grandchildren came together here. We all gathered around his bed and conducted a "Blessing of One Who Draws Near to Death"[38] service that was given to us by Sally, our hospice volunteer and written by Joyce Rupp. It is a beautiful service. In this service we shared our love and gratitude, freed him to take leave of us as his time draws near, and blessed his head, his eyes, his ears, his mouth, his hands, his feet, and his heart. Each member shared in the service. Each part ended with, "You will always be a part of our hearts. Go in peace." We began by singing one of Loren's favorite hymns, "Lord of All Hopefulness," and concluded with, "May the longtime sun shine upon you, all love surround you, and the pure light within you guide you on your way home" (a blessing sung at ARC when guests depart) and *Silent Night.* At the conclusion of the short service, Loren said in a strong voice, "Goodbye, my beloved family. I love you all very much."

We were all deeply touched by the intimate service and especially by Loren's farewell.

"May the angels of hope take you by the hand and lead you home."

[38] This beautiful service can be found in Joyce Rupp's book, *Out of the Ordinary: Prayers, Poems and Reflections for Every Season.*

Wednesday, December 9, 2009

We seem to be in the transition phase of this "laboring process." Loren is moving from one place to another. Some transitions are smooth and easy, others are more complex and challenging; it is always a movement to something new. Sometimes it feels like we are straddling two worlds. That becomes the hard work, the challenge. Loren has said all his goodbyes, and he has prayed, "Come, Lord Jesus, come." We wait with him these days. He assures us, "I trust the process. I'm confident in the process. It will work its way out. In brokenness will come justice. God is justice." These words were his response to the question, "Are you peaceful?"

We again pray for a peaceful night and a peaceful transition for Loren when that moment arrives. Your prayers and kind words sustain us daily.

Thursday, December 10, 2009

Loren has been to the heights and to the depths this day. This time has often been described as being on a roller coaster. Loren has seen the most beautiful and the most terrible in his journey today. Even though his images and metaphors are not always understood by us, the family has been very present to him, loving him through the challenges of this great mystery of dying.

Tonight I accompanied Mary, Dan, and granddaughter Siri to the Concordia[39] Christmas concert at Orchestra

[39] Concordia College is located in Moorhead, Minnesota. The school's choirs host their annual Christmas concert in Moorhead with a concert also given each year at Orchestra Hall in downtown Minneapolis.

Hall. It was exceptionally beautiful and meaningful to me. I would like to end my entry tonight with a prayer from the concert, which I would like to say for Loren.

> O loving Savior, draw your gentle arms around me, and fold me in your tender care. Calm the stirring of my trembling hands, silence the clangor of my angry voice; lighten the shadows of my wintry eyes. O spring of loving-kindness, nurture me in your grace, sustain me in my doubt, hold me in my weakness. Let me drink from your living waters, and taste your food of light. Root me, grow me, 'til I flower, teach me, love me, lead me to you.

Friday, December 11, 2009

We continue to watch and wait with Loren. In the early morning hours, he felt confused and agitated. This continued on and off until late morning, when the hospice chaplain[40] paid a visit. The chaplain helped talk through some of the confusion Loren was experiencing, which helped still and quiet him together with the help of pain and anxiety medications. The remainder of the day has been calm and quiet, with Loren being more the Loren we know and love. He has been resting comfortably since.

He is considerably weaker but also more peaceful. We know this is a time of relinquishment and letting go. To a once active, passionate man, this is not always easy. Each of the children and spouses has tended Loren

[40] Steve

with great compassion, understanding, tenderness, and love. I could not ask for more. They have been a great support to Loren and to me. Although this has been a challenging time, it has also deepened relationships with one another in a special way.

We feel such support and encouragement through your CaringBridge entries. Thank you everyone.

Saturday, December 12, 2009

Again it has been a day that ranged from peacefulness to struggle, from reality to unreality. At times, we as a family struggle over how best to comfort, encourage, and support Loren. The wonderful hospice medical aide came this morning and bathed Loren, lotioned and powdered his body, making him as comfortable as possible. Later in the day, a hospice nurse stopped by to evaluate the medications we are giving and to help us with our care giving.

Dying, like birthing, can be a painful and arduous journey. We pray for understanding, gentleness, and compassion in our care giving, knowing that Loren is ready, willing, and wanting to move to his final home. At one point he was asked if he has fear of dying. He replied, "No, rather I have fear of living." As Loren has prayed, so we too pray this night, "Come, Lord Jesus, come."

Sunday, December 13, 2009

My dad had a very good day today, and most important, he was less agitated than the past few days. We were able to get him out of bed and into his living room chair for the first time in a week. My sister Becky and I also gave him a "tour" (from his wheelchair) of the artwork by Harry Nurmet in Mom and Dad's apartment. When we came across a framed cross-stitch,[41] I asked, "Who made this?" He replied, "I think that was me."

Other highlights of the day include four chocolate malt servings, a phone call from his sister-in-law Jean, listening to Handel's *Messiah*, and my Mom and I reading Ted Kennedy's autobiography, *True Compass*, to Loren.

All in all, a full day filled with gratitude!

~ *Mark (child #2)*

Monday, December 14, 2009

The spurt of energy we experienced from Loren yesterday was short-lived. Beginning last evening and through the night, Loren was much calmer and more of the person we know; however, he is like the psalmist, pleading with God to take him home, to release him. His laments are so heartfelt, so earnest and genuine. At his request, I too, prayed for his release and homecoming into the arms of a welcoming God.

With the third candle of Advent[42] lit, we are slowly moving into more light—into that "Full Light" we have been promised.

---

[41] Embroidered by Loren

[42] Many Christians use Advent wreaths during the four-week period before Christmas. The wreath consists of four candles set into a circle of greenery. In the center is a fifth candle. Each of the four candles represents one millennium of waiting during the traditional 4,000 years from God's Biblical promise to Abraham to

Tuesday, December 15, 2009

Loren had a visit from the hospice music therapist this morning. She played a wonderful selection[43] of Christmas and Advent hymns on her gentle-sounding instrument, humming along with some of the songs. It was very soothing and greatly appreciated by Loren. We have had soft classical music playing much of the day. Loren has always loved good music. This afternoon the hospice home health aide came and bathed and freshened him with lotion and powder and made him comfortable. The health aides are very skilled and knowledgeable in ways to care for and comfort the ill. He also had a brief hello from two good friends, and of course, one or more of the family is always here.

Loren's spirit is very ready and prepared to move on to a better place; however, his physical body is not as willing or ready. Medication has helped to clear Loren's brain; he is now more his gentle, grateful self. What is most amazing to us and to the nurses and doctors is how active, productive, and articulate his mind still is. He still has plans for how some good might be brought to the world.

Wednesday, December 16, 2009

We continue to watch and wait with Loren. The hospice doctor changed one of Loren's medications today, with

send a redeemer until the arrival on Christmas of Jesus. During the first week of Advent, one candle is lit. During the second, two candles are lit, and so on. On Christmas, all five candles are lit.

[43] On a portable keyboard

the hope that it will help him rest better at night. The past few nights have been restless, with only short periods of sleep. Loren spent most of today in the living room in his recliner/lift chair. This morning the brilliant sun streamed into the living room where he sat, giving such brightness, as well as warmth, to the room.

Loren's body appears to be weaker, yet his resilience is remarkable. His voice is also weaker but so gentle and kind, at the same time questioning and struggling with the long process. We are so glad we can care for him at home in this frail and tender time.

Last Sunday morning I heard the beautiful Bach cantata *Herr Christ, der Einz'ge Gottes Sohn (Lord Christ, the Only Son of God)* at our daughter and son-in-law's church.[44] The soprano recitative and the bass aria reflect for me the journey we have been making with Loren these past many weeks: "O give me, Lord my God, your righteous guidance; without you I can have no light. In human sinfulness and might I err in disobedience. But when you, O Lord, do surround me and lead me with your eyes ever securely, my journey will be blest and lead to heaven's rest."

And from the aria: "This way, that way, wandering, faltering, I am lost without your hand. Walk with me, my Savior God. Leave me not in need and struggling. Grant that I may know your guidance, leading me to heaven's radiance."

---

[44] Our daughter Mary and son-in-law Dan serve as pastors at Grace University Lutheran Church.

Thursday, December 17, 2009

Loren had a 10-hour sleep last night, and until late afternoon he was only minimally engaged. He communicated very little and seemed very weak, giving us and the hospice nurse the impression that death was near. Later this afternoon he surprised us all by becoming more energized and communicating with each of the family that came. Many of the family gathered here for dinner and to be with Loren. Granddaughter Siri played beautiful piano music for him, which he enjoyed immensely.

A hospice nurse visited and provided us with helpful information in signs to watch for and ways to best care for Loren in the dying process.[45]

In a conversation Loren and I had earlier in the evening, he said something like, "The best word is often hidden in the last word. The most beautiful is often hidden in the most terrible, the most trying times."

We seek to embrace both the trying times, as well as the beautiful and precious moments.

Friday, December 18, 2009

Dad's day started with the question, "I'm wondering what the reaction will be today?" When asked, "The reaction to what?" he replied, "The reaction to prejudice." Even as Dad lies in bed, his body becoming weaker, his

---

[45] Some signs include loss of appetite, increased sleeping, confusion, restlessness and agitation, and changes in breathing, temperature, and skin color.

mind remains active and focused on issues that are important to him.

As the day progressed, his energy seemed to wane, and he spent more time resting. At one point he said to me, "Goodbye, Becky." I asked him if it felt like he was going, and he said, "Yes I do." Later today he told Mom, "It's hard—it's so hard."

We pray for peace for Dad in his body, mind, and spirit.
~ Becky (child #4)

Saturday, December 19, 2009

Yes, the veil between life and death is very thin. For us, this is a precious time, a waiting time, a thanksgiving time and also a difficult time. We keep whispering in Loren's ear that he is loved so very much, that we will miss him terribly, but that we also release him into the arms of a loving, welcoming God. I asked him this morning if he was nearing the end of his journey here on earth and he nodded ever so slightly in the affirmative.

He is less responsive, but appears peaceful. Loren was awake briefly early this morning and again briefly this evening when he took some juice, water, and malted milk.

As we watch and wait, we remember and rejoice, we cry and we laugh. Life is filled with paradoxes. We hold on to the promise that darkness will not be the last Word. I believe Loren is moving into the mystery of new life.

Sunday, December 20, 2009

God is a God of surprises! We have been surprised again and again these past weeks, including this past day! From a day of unresponsiveness for much of yesterday, we have seen a Loren who has since engaged with family with an active mind and even wit and humor. He eagerly listened to a series of Christmas stories from the *New York Times* read to him today. In response to one of the stories about someone being "Mona Lisa-ed," he said, "I didn't know that Mona Lisa could be used as a verb."

This afternoon Lisa asked Loren if he had any words to describe how he felt. She said she was curious about what he must physically feel like, and again she and we were surprised by his response. "Suspended in grace, and dependent on love."

Tonight he has been telling us of his gratitude for each member of the family and how ready he is to die. He wondered what the appropriate approach to God would be since he didn't want to "tell God what to do." He wants to be open, so "Oh, yes, oh, yes" has become his prayer.

We are enjoying his heartfelt conversations, his honesty, his concern for others, his wit and humor, and his graciousness. Tomorrow we will be open to more surprises.

Monday, December 21, 2009

The surprises continue. After a good night's rest, Loren awoke with energy, clarity of mind, and the desire to share some personal experiences he has had in the dying process. He also made requests that he wanted the family to understand and carry through. We promised that we would respect and honor his wishes. We have had some of our most profound and deeply spiritual talks with Loren today, all of which were initiated by him. We concluded that the dying process has been a rich learning and growing experience for each of us in the family, as well as for Loren himself. He said the process is a "theological goldmine" and one to approach with great humility and honesty.

Loren also had a long and beautiful conversation with Siri and Peder, his grandchildren, and a visit from his great-granddaughter Lucy.

A group of fifteen carolers stopped by this evening and sang several beautiful carols in full, rich harmony. What a gift to us and so very much appreciated by Loren.

Loren is prepared and ready to die, unafraid and waiting to be received into the welcome of a loving, gracious God.

Tuesday, December 22, 2009

Today Loren had the "royal bath" from his wonderful home health aide,[46] who tends him with such care and skill. He also had a visit from a dear friend with whom there was deep sharing, time of prayer, and a poignant farewell. Various family members stopped by throughout the day, with each one having a meaningful and personal conversation with him.

---

[46] Donretha

Loren continues to speak of gratitude for his family, for all the opportunities and experiences he has known, and for life itself. However, he has said repeatedly that he is so ready now to step into the promised new life, but his body seems less willing and continues to keep going, despite being wracked with spreading cancer. Loren has fervently prayed to be able to leave this world of pain and travail, but we know that it is not in our hands to choose the day or the hour of our departure. We pray for patience for Loren and a spirit of love and gentleness for each of us in the family as we accompany him as far as we can. We have released him into God's care, despite our sadness and pain in doing so because he is prepared and desires this so much.

The waiting and preparation of Advent has taken on new meaning for us all as we now move into the realization and fullness of our waiting.

Wednesday, December 23, 2009

The human body is a complex and wonderful structure, full of mystery. Since his illness began, Loren's body has gone through a full range of responses, from intense pain to incredible joy, from unresponsiveness to total alertness, from confusion to clarity, from slurred speech to clear articulation. Although he is weaker, today he has had visits with family, hospice chaplain, and our pastor, recalling important events, people, and even quotes. In the midst of it all, he often offers us his unique sense of humor and wit.

His food intake has been limited to juice, water, and his favorite—malted milk—for several weeks now. The body is truly an amazing instrument that has resilience and enduring qualities that amaze us. Our journey has been a gift, a grace, a holy time that will be cherished and remembered by each member of the family for the rest of our lives.

Thursday, December 24, 2009

Beautiful Christmas music filled our home most of today. Loren enjoyed this so much. Today he has been more quiet and reflective. Two dear friends visited briefly, as did the hospice nurse. The family gathered here for Christmas Eve dinner prepared by Becky and Dan. Loren was helped to come to the living room, where he spent an hour or so; however, he grew very tired and was helped back to bed. His prayer would be answered if he could go to his eternal rest tonight. He is weary and very ready.

I conclude with a verse in a Christmas card we received from a friend. It was written by June Nyblade, a former missionary:

Alpha and Omega
Define the seasons of our lives.
First gasp of breath, a startled wail,
Through faltering steps, a sigh, farewell.
I'm the Alpha at creation's dawning.
I'm in a stable, new born, appearing

Each Christmas morning
As you celebrate my birth.
I am the Omega, promised ending
With love surrounding your life's
Ascending to a new beginning
Everlasting.

Friday, December 25, 2009

We have feasted on good music and superb concerts these past couple of days, on both radio and television, that have told the Christmas story in inspiring and beautiful ways. Loren has found such joy and comfort in the music. Where else in the world could we have the wealth of accomplished choirs and choral groups that we have in the Midwest?

Loren has had a relatively good day. His mind is alert and sharp; however, he is weaker and his intake is quite limited—water, ice chips, and other selected juices.

The family came again late afternoon bearing food, gifts, and good cheer. We sang carols around Loren's bed before we had another feast. Today Loren preferred to remain in his bed, with family members going in and out of the bedroom to talk or just stay with him. We see each day as a gift that we treasure and try to make the most of.

And so we pray that the gift of Love born at Christmastime will find a home in our hearts and in our world.

Saturday, December 26, 2009

The following is taken from a discussion I had with Loren this evening and his dictation to me.

Your messages have been nurturing, inspiring, and endearing. As I have lain here the past couple of days, I have wondered why there seems to be a delay in my journey to eternity. One possible reason was to be able to listen to Bill Moyers's magnificent documentary[47] Friday evening on public television. The program had a great deal to do with mindfulness. The program was actually about the modern dance performance entitled *Fondly Do We Hope . . . Fervently Do We Pray*, written by Bill T. Jones, depicting the life and work of President Abraham Lincoln. I was intrigued about his approach to Lincoln as a person of great mindfulness as he wrestled with the issue of slavery, and beyond that at a deeper level, with the issue of being himself. How wonderful, I thought, that still in my lifetime one might witness such public wrestling with matters of the soul. There is hope for our nation, I thought, that such discussions of matters of the heart can take place in the public square. I could depart this life with a greater degree of comfort and hope to know that this level of public discussion—drama and public performance—was able to take place. If, as we so often experienced at ARC, this quality of sharing could multiply, I would

[47] TV series Bill Moyer's Journal took a unique look at our nation's sixteenth president—through the eyes of critically acclaimed veteran dance artist Bill T. Jones. Through dance, Jones reimagines a young Lincoln in his formative years.

indeed be much encouraged upon my departure. I especially appreciate the breadth and inclusiveness of Moyers's and artist Jones's approach because I leave this world increasingly persuaded that God is more inclusive than I have ever been able to imagine in my lifetime.

Jesus is present in this world in places and forms beyond that which we humans could ever imagine. It is a vast company—it takes one's breath away.

I thank each one of you who over the years has nudged me along this way.

With love and gratitude,
~ *Loren (and Ruth)*

Sunday, December 27, 2009

This morning and early afternoon, Loren has had poignant conversations with family members on the meaningful, personal, and surprising experiences he has had in the dying process. He has traveled a great distance in his journey and has made wonderful discoveries that are not only beliefs but personal experiences of faith that ring true for him in a deeper way. "I am overwhelmed by Jesus' love; there are no boundaries to Christ's love and inclusiveness."

This morning Loren watched a DVD on the computer called *Note on Note*, a story explaining the care and precision that goes into building a Steinway piano. Loren was deeply moved by this documentary. The slow and painstaking process that is adhered to finally ends in a finished product of great and lasting quality.

Later in the afternoon, there was a change for Loren. He developed serious pain, confusion, and unsettledness, which required more medication. And so we try to deal with the many changes that come with as much understanding and compassion as we can. Loren is a unique person, and we know his dying process will be unique. We hold onto the promise that God is our refuge and strength.

Monday, December 28, 2009

One is brought to the heights and to the depths in the dying process; it is not a steady, routine, or predictable process. As soon as we think we are entering upon a regular schedule, new challenges or surprises enter in to change that. The capacity for the body to live can be very strong; at the same time, the desire to move on to the new life that has been promised is equally strong. The dying process is surely akin to the birthing process, which can elicit varying length and intensity of pain, struggle, resistance, reward, and joy.

Today has been for Loren "a dark night of the soul," as he put it. However, I believe that when one stays with the darkness or impasse rather than aborting it or fleeing from it, morning does come, and we are surprised by joy. The prayer of the family is that he will come to experience a peace that passes human understanding.

Tuesday, December 29, 2009

This has been a quiet day of watching and waiting with Loren. He has been in a deep sleep since last evening beginning at 9:30, with only brief moments of opening his eyes. He has recognized everyone he has seen today but quickly drops off to sleep again. He indicated that he wanted it quiet rather than have conversation or music. However, this evening around 8:00, he awoke and requested hearing the CaringBridge entries. After hearing several entries, he expressed a desire to also share something. The following is what Loren dictated to me.

> Your daily messages are life-giving, especially in the midst of dying. If someone asks me at the end of this journey what sustained me, I would reply, the wisdom that so many friends, as well as strangers, were willing to share. In the midst of my own questioning, discovering this mutuality is in its own way life-nourishing; powerful pedagogy indeed!

Loren appears very much at peace and I am grateful. Today I have whispered in his ear, "I love you, go in peace. Go gently into the night." May his transition be peaceful.

With gratitude and love,
~ *Loren and Ruth*

Wednesday, December 30, 2009

From the day we first learned that there would be no possible cure, only palliative treatment[48] for Loren and his cancer, there has been incredible learning going on for our family regarding the dying process, or I might say, the "birthing" new life process. We as a family have been privileged to walk this road with Loren, to care for him in all his ups and downs, to converse with him, to sit in silence with him, to pray with him, to sing with him and for him, to hold him, to cry with him, to laugh with him, to learn from him. It has been a learning for us that is precious, personal, poignant, and surprising. As we can testify, dying involves hard work, and Loren has been working hard. He is very ready and willing to move on to the new life; however, his body is remarkably strong and resilient and does not seem as ready.

At one point when I came into the bedroom today, Loren said, "I feel something is about to happen." I asked him if he felt he was entering into another world or another space and he replied, "Into the 'Real World'—don't let anyone tell you it's not the 'Real World.'"

At another time he acknowledged that he was so confused. He seemed to know where he was and the time of year, but he was confused about time. When one is straddling two worlds at times, I can imagine that our understanding of time is not the same as one experiences it in the promised new life. At these special moments, it feels like an intrusion for me to ask too many questions, for it seems to be a sacred and personal time.

---

[48] Also called comfort care

We feel so nurtured, supported, and loved through your inspiring and personal CaringBridge entries, through your e-mails, through your cards, and through the many gestures and kindnesses we have received. Thank you! We are grateful!

Thursday, December 31, 2009

Loren has moments of complete clarity, and he also has moments that are not as clear or easily understood by him or by us. He remains so gentle and kind and is filled with gratitude for every kindness shown him. His passion for justice and peace even now continues.

A couple of days ago, we received a letter from a dear friend who sent us a description of faith written by Frederick Buechner.[49] I would like to share this with you as we watch and wait with Loren.

> Faith is different from theology because theology is reasoned, systematic, orderly, whereas faith is disorderly, intermittent and full of surprises. Faith is different from mysticism because mystics in their ecstasy become one with what faith can at most see only from afar. Faith is different from ethics because ethics is primarily concerned not, like faith, with our relationship to God but our relationship to each other. . . . Faith is homesickness. Faith is a lump in the throat. Faith is less a position *on* than a movement *toward*, less a sure thing than a hunch. Faith is waiting. Faith is journeying through space and through time.

---

[49] American writer and theologian

We are approaching the end of a year and the end of a decade on this cold "blue moon" evening.[50] As we witness this infrequent and unusual happening, we await an even more beautiful and mysterious event of transition for Loren, a wonderful new life for him that will be free of pain and struggle. Loren and I and the family send our gratitude to all of you for your beautiful CaringBridge entries with wishes for a New Year that moves closer to peace between and among peoples of all nations.

Friday, January 1, 2010

This afternoon Loren experienced "healing touch" from a most gifted Episcopal priest. She shared with Loren that she had a near-death experience herself as a young woman. She said it was a wonderful and beautiful experience; however, she was not ready at that time to leave this life. She reassured Loren that dying is not a fearful experience but a beautiful one. It is the waiting that is difficult and challenging. As humans we often try to process things through our minds rather than our hearts; even in dying we try to figure it out. Healing touch helps us to move to the heart and lessen the resistance to the love that God has available to all of us. Loren was able to feel from his heart the love that surrounds him this afternoon. It was a sacred and beautiful time for Loren and for each family member who was present at the time. We feel we have been gifted again and again in this journey.

---

[50] The second full moon of a single calendar month; figuratively, a very rare event

As we begin the new year, we trust that for however much time we are granted with Loren, we will be given the strength, the compassion, the gentleness to care for him and to accompany him as far as we can. We pray that Loren will be granted a peaceful transition into the beautiful new life he has been promised.

Saturday, January 2, 2010

When Loren awoke this morning after an 11-hour sound sleep, I said, "Good morning, Sweetheart."

He replied ever so softly, "Good morning, Sweetheart. It's a beautiful, perfect day!"

"Did you have a good sleep?" I said.

"It was magnificent," he replied. He went on to say that he found it difficult to arrive at the right words to describe fully what he really was experiencing.

After a rather brief conversation, Loren fell asleep again and slept much of the day. In the late afternoon, he awoke and again fully engaged with the family members who were here. He has an amazing ability to arise from a long, deep sleep and enter rather quickly into an articulate, meaningful conversation, periodically offering his whimsical and humorous quips. His comebacks and resilience are a wonder to us, as well as to the hospice people.

Loren appears very much at peace with a joyful spirit and a readiness to enter into his new life completely. For this I am most grateful.

Sunday, January 3, 2010

We are realizing more than ever that life is a precious gift. As humans we have a strong will to live. Our survival skills speak to this intense desire. Our prayers often go in the direction of healing, health, safety, and wholeness. In recent days and weeks, however, Loren has prayed fervently that he be released from this life into the loving arms of a gracious God and that he be able to move on to what God has promised and prepared for him. His prayer has been, "Come, Lord Jesus, come quickly." We die so that we may live; the great paradox! We are living in the midst of paradox. This great paradox will not be fully understood until we cross that final threshold. At times these days, it feels like Loren is living in the space between heaven and earth, "suspended in grace and held by love" as he so beautifully articulated some weeks ago.

In these weeks of keeping vigil with Loren, death has taken on a different face—a face more welcoming and less foreboding, more gracious and less fearful, more natural and less frightening.

Monday, January 4, 2010

Last evening Loren asked me to call a colleague and friend of his on the telephone. The friend surprised us by offering to come in person rather than visit on the phone. They spent a wonderful hour together, conversing about many things, spending time in silence, and praying. I joined them in the last part of their visit. We both knelt at Loren's bed in silence and prayer. It was a beautiful time that I believe enabled Loren to have a very peaceful night's sleep. There is so much we do not know about the power of silence to still the restless, waiting heart.

Loren has taken primarily only water and a little orange-juice-and-7up combination for the past several weeks. He has had considerable weight loss but remains his gentle, loving self. He continues to have wonderful, stimulating conversations with family members. He is definitely as unique in his dying as he has been unique in his living; however, he is moving slowly and gently into decline.

We have had visits from the massage therapist, the hospice nurse, and the home health aide today, all of whom have tended Loren with such gentleness, skill, and compassion.

The third verse from the hymn "Love Has Come" is my closing word tonight.

> Love has come and never will leave us! Love is life everlasting and free. Love is Jesus within and among us. Love is the peace our hearts are seeking. Love! Love! Love is the gift of Christmas. Love! Praise to you, God on high!

Tuesday, January 5, 2010

Loren had a good night, and he has had good moments of visiting today with family members who have come and gone throughout the day. It is so amazing that in his wakeful moments, he remains so vital and articulate, despite the wasting of his body.

Granddaughter Jenny came this evening and gave Loren a foot massage, which he enjoyed so much. This time not only provided helpful, soothing touch for Loren but also an opportunity to spend time visiting with his granddaughter.

Although death seems to hover near at times, we do not know the day or the hour God will choose. Loren has been questioning and wondering why he has not been called to his eternal home, when spiritually and emotionally he is so ready. We give a similar response to him with each questioning—we do not know the day or the hour. It is in God's timing, not ours. Of course Loren knows this too; however, it does not stop the wondering.

Despite the unpredictability of this journey, Loren continues to remain immensely grateful for every kindness rendered him, every family member, every blessing he has received in life. He continues to give thanks for a rich and full life, blessed in abundance. We as family feel blessed to care for Loren and to continue meaningful and wonderful conversations with him.

Wednesday, January 6, 2010

Today we move into another season of the church year in our waiting and watching with Loren. Epiphany,[51] the season of light and revelation, has been experienced

---

[51] In the Christian tradition, Epiphany is the manifestation of God in human form (Jesus) and is traditionally considered the day the three wise men (magi) visited Jesus in Bethlehem with their gifts of gold, frankincense, and myrrh. The term *epiphany* has come to have the broader meaning of "realization," "sudden insight," or "revelation."

by Loren and by us as family again and again in this journey. When we have been uncertain or fearful, we have experienced enough light to bring us to the next point. We do not see far, but the light is sufficient for the next step. As we boldly take each step, enough light is provided. The entire path is not yet illuminated for Loren or for us, but as we move with confidence, the light appears as we need it.

Loren has had long periods of sleep today, as well as wakeful moments when he is fully engaged. He has been recalling many past experiences and people he has worked with or has known, and he recalls with gratitude what they have meant to him, how they have helped him, or what they did together. His recall of past experiences and stories continues to amaze us. We are grateful to hear these stories (sometimes not for the first time). He brings a deep concern for the people we have forgotten, excluded, or marginalized in our church and in our society.

Thursday, January 7, 2010

What I share tonight might be considered on the lighter side; of course Loren will soon discover what heaven really is like. I believe God has a sense of humor (wouldn't God have to, in dealing with humans?) and invites us to imagine and dream. There has been a great deal of curiosity about what heaven will be like. Loren awoke this afternoon after a long rest and shared with me that he had just experienced heaven—there was an endless supply of chocolate ice cream, not dark chocolate but a lighter brand. "Would that be sacrilegious?" he wondered.

"No," I said, "I think God would be delighted!"

Associating ice cream (especially chocolate malted milk) with heaven perhaps originated in his youth he says. He remembers going to the Rush River Church in Wisconsin as a child, his parent's home church, for church picnics and where homemade ice cream was served in abundance together with ice-cold watermelon. Loren loves to fantasize about heaven. Curiosity has always been a strong component of Loren's makeup and still remains a compelling force.

Friday, January 8, 2010

It has been said, "Wait, and the opportunity will come." Loren continues to wonder why his end on earth is so long in coming. "Lord, what do you have in mind by stretching this out so long?" he asks of God. Might there still be something for him to do?

After hearing about a letter in yesterday's [Minneapolis] *Star Tribune* in regard to disagreement by some with the vote taken last summer at the ELCA General Assembly regarding GLBT[52] folk,[53] Loren wondered if this might be his opportunity. The unwillingness of many to accept

---

[52] Gay, lesbian, bisexual, and transgendered

[53] Each year, representatives of the ELCA from various parts of the country gather at a national assembly. In August 2009, the national ELCA assembly voted to allow all gay and lesbian people in monogamous relationships to be ordained as clergy in the ELCA. Before that, only gay and lesbian people who were celibate could be ordained.

the August majority vote to include partnered GLBT folk in ordained ministry in the ELCA was sad and disappointing to us. The thought occurred to Loren as he lay waiting to die that this might be the moment, the opportunity for him to make a bold statement regarding this issue. This special time of the past three months has opened him (and all of us) to the expansive and inclusive love of God. He believes deeply that the intention of God is to bring people together, to include, not exclude, people. He believes we have a gospel of Good News, which is Good News for all people God has created, not just some.

God is an inclusive God, a God of unconditional love, a God of abundant grace. Loren, and we his family, believe that the same generosity of unconditional love and grace that he and we have experienced is there for all of God's children, especially in this instance—the GLBT people who have often been judged and targeted so shamefully by the church and society and who have waited so long for justice.

With the stamp of God's image imprinted on every person in creation, every person deserves to experience the fullness of God's love and the fullness of his or her individual calling and gifts.

Our hope lies in spreading God's unconditional love and refusing the path of violence, judgment, or indifference.

Saturday, January 9, 2010

Although it may sound surprising to hear, this week has seemed to have a degree of "normalcy" to it. The dying process is very much a part of living—living and dying blend into one. We the family and caregivers of Loren have had a full night's sleep the past six nights, and the days have been quite predictable. During the day, Loren has periods of sleep, and when he is awake he is fully awake, interacting with whoever is here in thoughtful and meaningful ways.

Other than his body being very weak and very thin, he is more alert in his awake times than he has been in some weeks. We cannot explain this type of mental and communication alertness, since he has not had any food to speak of for several weeks. His principal diet has been juice and water. Yesterday and today he tried a few spoons of chicken noodle soup, but that has been the extent of real food. He seems to have a residual storehouse of energy, alertness, and presence that defies even the hospice people.

Today he requested that we telephone a few of his close friends and colleagues to have a conversation with them. In the past two days, he has spoken with several. He expresses great gratitude for these conversations, which he would not have been able to have a short time ago. Loren finds himself growing into deeper and more intimate relationship with family and friends. He has been particularly grateful for the conversations with the grandchildren. He feels there is a depth and honesty now to these conversations. These days one gets more quickly to the heart of the matter, to the important issues of life.

On the one hand he is very patient with his family and caregivers; however, on the other hand he is very impatient that this dying process is taking so long. We can only comfort him and assure him that we all appreciate the added, unexpected time we have with him. We know one thing for certain—we are not in charge!

Sunday, January 10, 2010

The Isaiah text for today[54] is very beautiful and gives much assurance and comfort in these days of watching and waiting:

Do not fear, for I have redeemed you;
I have called you by name, you are mine.
When you pass through the waters, I will be with you;
and through the rivers, they shall not overwhelm you;
when you walk through fire you shall not be burned. . . .
Do not fear, for I am with you. . . .

What consolation and reassurance this text is for Loren and me. To know that we are intimately known, loved, and addressed by a gracious God is a precious gift.

Monday, January 11, 2010

Although Loren's body is very weak, his mind is strong and clear. He had a desire, understandably, to see some different scenery other than just our bedroom. Son-in-law Dan, granddaughter Siri, and friend Brent

---

[54] From Isaiah chapter 43, verses 1–2, 5

responded to his wish, and he was lifted into the wheelchair and wheeled around the apartment. The bright light coming into our many large windows on this January morning was both stimulating and pleasant for Loren. Siri played the piano, and Brent sang in his beautiful tenor voice. Even great-granddaughter Lucy sang for him. It was lovely. He sat up for 15 to 20 minutes.

Earlier this morning Loren requested to listen to the news, something he has not been interested in for some time. After a short while, he turned the TV off and said to Mary, our daughter, "There is so much junk on TV; there is nothing inspiring. We don't have to go to hell—we are already in it!" In response to a family member reflecting on his deep thoughts, he responded, "Most of my life I've been paid to think these 'deep thoughts.'"

His energetic mind keeps working, even though the rest of his body is becoming more sensitive even to ordinary touch. We are learning how to announce every move we plan with him and then to be ever so gentle in our movements. He is peaceful and ready to depart this life, though impatient with the delay.

Tuesday, January 12, 2010

As the dying process continues, various areas of the body become more sensitive to touch and movement. As caregivers we work with slow and gentle movements when we change Loren's position in bed or turn him. Despite his limitations these days, Loren remains patient and grateful to us for every kindness rendered. His pain and discomfort are managed with medication; however, some days seem very long to him. We are grateful to the hospice people for the counsel, understanding, and expertise we receive from them to guide us through whatever situation in which we find ourselves.

Although some moments are trying, Loren meets each new challenge with calmness and grace. Today he has enjoyed being read to and occasionally watching a good program on TV. He also enjoyed a visit from the hospice chaplain today and the bath and special treatment he received from his home health aide. He has asked me to thank the many, many friends who have written daily entries in the CaringBridge guestbook. Every day he looks forward to the messages and enjoys hearing them read and reread. Your words have been words of great encouragement, comfort, and support to him and all of us.

We know we cannot hurry or stop the dying process. We pray for patience, understanding, and gentleness as we continue on this journey.

Wednesday, January 13, 2010

It is a great mystery why so many good people fervently pray to live and be spared death and others pray equally fervently to be taken to their final home, as Loren has prayed. Another great mystery for us in the family is that as his body becomes weaker and frailer, his cognitive skills and awareness have not diminished. The complexities and beauty of the human body and spirit are a marvel—"and God saw everything he [God] had made, and indeed, it was very good."[55]

I am very grateful that we have been able to care for Loren at home. This was his wish. This care would not have been possible without the overwhelming and constant support of our family. We have all learned so much and grown so much in our relationship with each other. We feel enormously blessed to have had this time and many in-depth conversations with Loren. Despite the sometimes demanding responsibilities and unpredictability of this passage, to accompany Loren on this, his most significant journey, has been a gift we will hold forever.

Thursday, January 14, 2010

Loren quoted the following words to me this afternoon for the evening journal entry.

> Thank you for the rich memories that your reflections bring, which we look forward to as a daily homecoming, preparing us for that final homecoming when at last there will be no more place to go, for I will be at that final destination of the human spirit where we are all at home and at peace with one another. Thank you for your encouragement.
>
> Peace and love,
> ~ *Loren*

---

[55] Genesis 1:31

Friday, January 15, 2010

A great part of each day goes by uneventfully as we go about the daily tasks of care and comfort-giving for Loren. Then we are sometimes surprised by a new pain or discomfort that develops for him. We try our best to attend to these challenges. Even though we are not expert on what to do in these changing events, we feel we have gained a degree of understanding as to what works and what does not work for Loren. The hospice people give excellent counsel and often encourage us by telling us that at times we may be the ones who know best what works and what does not.

Today Loren has been sleeping a great deal, but when he awoke early evening, he shared a beautiful dream he had. He dreamt that Becketwood was a small, rural parish where he was a member and where he was being cared for. It was a Sunday. He dreamt that a contest was being held that Sunday in which churches throughout the synod were competing in a hymn contest that dealt with rhyme, word, meter, and all the elements one would look for in a hymn contest. When I came into the bedroom, he assumed that I was just returning from that worship service where the competing hymns were shared. Our local parish (Becketwood) won the contest with the spectacular words used in the hymn. The prize was one million dollars! When he awoke, the dream seemed so real to him. He was so excited. He was amazed that I did not show greater enthusiasm. He was greatly disappointed at my lack of excitement, which he thought the prize surely warranted. A while later when I brought him his usual drink of orange-juice-and-7up mix, he said, "Is that all the better you can do after such a big win?"

Loren's imagination is still active.

Saturday, January 16, 2010

As the days go by, we notice greater sensitivity to touch and weight developing in certain parts of Loren's body, particularly his feet and legs. We try to ease the weight of the bed covers by creating a makeshift tent over his feet. He has also been sleeping more the past couple of days. For the most part, Loren's pain and discomfort are managed by the current medication regime he is on, thanks to the hospice people.

Granddaughter Siri stayed overnight last night, and today we had a wonderful visit from our niece and nephew from Fargo who drove down just for today and spent several hours with us. Loren was particularly pleased to see them and grateful for their visit. Other family members also stopped by today.

Tonight as I reflect on our life together, I am very thankful for 57 and one half years of shared love and partnership. We have been blessed in abundance with family, friends, shared values and work, many good experiences, and wonderful opportunities. We have a bank of wonderful memories. We could not have asked for more.

Sunday, January 17, 2010

This has been a quiet Sabbath day. Loren has been developing greater sensitivity in his legs, feet, and lower back. It is with slow and careful movements that we change his position in bed and care for him. He has been sleeping well at night and sleeping more during the day. When he is awake, however, he is engaged with family and even interested in listening to news.

The news from Haiti,[56] in particular, has been overwhelming. The destruction, devastation, and enormous suffering of so many people is heart wrenching.

It is difficult to comprehend the extent and far-reaching destruction of this poor country and the terrible anguish and despair the people must feel.

And so tonight we pray for life and relief for all people who are hungry, homeless, or abandoned, and we pray for those who desire to be released from this life, that they all may feel the tender embrace and presence of a compassionate and loving God.

Monday, January 18, 2010

It is difficult to see a loved one in pain or anguish. Today Loren has had times of confusion, which has disturbed him and raised his anxiety level. His pain seemed also to be at an increased level. The home health aide came for Loren's bath and personal care. Later in the

---

[56] On January 12, 2010, an earthquake with a magnitude of 7.0 on the Richter scale devastated much of Haiti in the area around the capital city, Port au Prince.

afternoon we had a visit from the hospice doctor and our regular hospice nurse. They advised us regarding a slight change in the medication regime and spoke at length with Loren, giving him reassurance. The doctor carefully explained what happens to the body in the dying process. Loren was reassured that he would not have to try to figure things out anymore but simply try to relax his mind and rest in the love of his family and in the love of God. For one who has always had an active and problem-solving mind, it is difficult and can be scary to realize that one's mental capacities may not be working at the same level as previously experienced.

The visit was very calming and helpful to Loren. After a troubling day, we are grateful he is entering sleep peacefully. "Now the day is over, night is drawing nigh . . .," and continued in Loren's words, ". . . but a new morning awaits us."

Tuesday, January 19, 2010

Today was a surprising contrast from yesterday. Loren slept the entire night waking for one hour this morning to receive his medications and be washed, turned, and made comfortable. He fell asleep again after an hour and slept until 4:00 this afternoon. Upon waking and after he became clear as to time, date, and place, he again became fully engaged, alert, and lucid with family members and with a friend who stopped by. He also fully engaged with our pastor, who visited him later this afternoon. The resilience and ability to rebound of this man amazes us all.

In his conversations Loren continues to show interest in and concerns for matters that reach beyond his personal sphere. His mind continues to spin dreams, create ideas, and solve problems.

This journey has had its highs and lows, its smooth places and its rough spots, its encouraging moments and its challenging times. We have learned so much and gained many new insights in this passage from life on earth to Life forever.

Wednesday, January 20, 2010

This journey has opened up many gifts and discoveries, not only regarding the dying process, but other important life learnings, as well. We believe it is through challenging times that we learn the most, perhaps because in these times we are more ready to listen and learn. One does not elect these emotional and challenging experiences; however, when they happen, they surprise us by becoming transforming gifts. What we thought was death turns out to be life, and what we thought was the end turns out to be the beginning. This is God's magnificent gift when we come to the last word! It is life giving, life renewing, life restoring.

Simply beyond description and imagination—it is incomprehensible, unconditional, and meant for all!

Thursday, January 21, 2010

For Loren the dying process has been a slow and gradual fading; for others death comes quickly and with little warning. This journey clearly demonstrates the uniqueness and individuality of each person. It also becomes a stark reminder that we are not in charge of our endings or our beginnings.

As we are granted more time, we are also granted more surprising gifts. The gifts come in many unexpected ways—visits, phone calls, conversations, encounters, understandings, insights, gestures of kindness, and more. As long as we are granted life, we are granted peace and purpose for each day.

Friday, January 22, 2010

Loren remains much the same, with his body growing gradually weaker, but his mind is still strong. He has been confined to his bed for some time now, and although that is difficult, we hold on to the incredible promise that all things work together for good.

With that in mind, I want to share a few thoughts on gratitude. This may seem absurd at this difficult time; however, we are encouraged in Scripture to give thanks in all circumstances, including the most difficult times. Especially at these times, God is with us, loving us, waiting for us, holding us up. Even the difficult times become a time of special growth in faith for which we can give thanks.

Julian of Norwich[57] once said, "The fullness of joy is to behold God in everything."

---

[57] A fourteenth-century English mystic and recluse. At age 30, Julian had a sequence of intense visions of Jesus, which she wrote about in her book *Sixteen Revelations of Divine Love.*

Saturday, January 23, 2010

Last evening we watched parts of the international telethon *Hope for Haiti Now.* This benefit lifted up the critical needs of the Haitian people, featuring celebrities and musicians who shared the Haitian stories. We were touched by many of the comments, stories, and songs. As we were preparing for the night, Loren asked me to "pray for peace in this troubled world."

I was reminded of the World Peace Prayer, which I leave with you. This is a prayer we have sung every day at the conclusion of the noon meal at the ARC Retreat Center since its early history. Unfortunately, I do not know the author or source. I first learned of this prayer and the practice suggested from the magazine *FOR*, from the Fellowship of Reconciliation, the oldest interfaith peace organization committed to nonviolence in the United States. It is suggested that this prayer be said or sung at noon around the world, thereby creating a chain of prayer for peace.

> *Lead me from death to life, from falsehood to truth.*
> *Lead me from despair to hope, from fear to trust.*
> *Lead me from hate to love, from war to peace.*
> *Let peace fill our hearts,*
> *Let peace fill our world,*
> *Let peace fill our universe. Amen.*

Sunday, January 24, 2010

Loren's condition continues much the same, although he is sleeping more and growing weaker and thinner.

He was happy to see Paul again today after he had been out of town for a couple of weeks.

One member of the family stays here with us every night, and someone is here most of every day. Loren and I are very grateful for the faithful presence, help, and support that our family has provided. Home hospice care would not have been possible for us without the generosity of the family. These times have provided many rich and poignant moments and conversations that we all treasure.

Whatever our situation is, there are riches to be discovered. We have had time to be together, time to be alone, time to be in silence, and time to be in conversation. Gerald May, a retreat leader, once said, "Life is holy, and the miraculous presence of God's grace flows through all of it." This has been our experience.

Monday, January 25, 2010

This morning Loren posed a very weighty question to Mary and me that surprised us. "If it were possible, would you be willing to start a new world, based on what we have learned so far? Would you be willing to suffer for that too?"

I was momentarily speechless. We wondered whether we really need to deal with such challenging and cosmic questions. My response to Loren's question was that I wondered if, given a chance, we humans would do any better the second time around. His questions cover such expansive and boundless subject matter. It does feel like

Loren will be challenging us to consider ways to better this world and the life of the people in it until his last moment.

Since he has been confined to his bed for some weeks, I asked him how his body felt. He said he was not as concerned with the deterioration of his body as he is that his mind may be slipping and not functioning as well as he would like. I assured him that although his body has deteriorated considerably, his mind shows very little diminishment and that he is unusually alert and aware. We can testify to that!

Today Loren was visited by the home health aide, who always makes him feel comfortable and relaxed, and by the hospice nurse. Later in the afternoon, a friend stopped by and sang for him and visited briefly. He was delighted by these visits but ready for a rest afterward.

Loren continues to amaze us with his reflections, his questions, his concerns, and his wit.

P.S.: Granddaughter Siri, who is staying with us tonight, sang Grampa to sleep with a beautiful lullaby.

Tuesday, January 26, 2010

This has been a very quiet day, with Loren spending a great portion of the time in a deep sleep. With the frequent changing of the guard here, with various family members, Loren still seems to be quite aware of who is here at any one time. Although he has prayed to be taken to his final home many times, especially earlier in his illness, we are amazed at his patience, graciousness, and continuing spirit of gratitude, plus demonstrating an acceptance of his illness. In his dying he is displaying a lasting legacy of gentleness and grace that will go with each of us forever.

One brief, sweet conversation we had late this afternoon was when I leaned over his bed and said, "I love you," and he responded with a very soft mouthing of, "I love you too. You said it first, but I thought it first."

Wednesday, January 27, 2010

When I sit down to a blank screen each evening, I sometimes wonder what I can write, after so many entries, that will be helpful and informative regarding Loren's condition. Interestingly enough, this challenge has become a reflective and thoughtful exercise for me to think about each day. I had not thought that it would be, but even though I sit down to a white screen at first, I find the process itself has become healing for me. Death has become more and more a part of life. The dying process no longer feels foreign or foreboding but almost friendly. When we are healthy and active, we claim life and want to live as fully as we can. When our bodies begin to deteriorate, and we no longer have the strength to live life actively, death takes on a more welcoming face. Loren is looking at his approaching death as a warm welcome that will allow him to join the host of family and friends who have preceded him.

I cannot say in enough ways how meaningful and encouraging your CaringBridge entries have been to Loren and me and our entire family. It brings a real sense of connection with each of you who have related to us in this way. Thank you so very much!

Thursday, January 28, 2010

Today I've been thinking about this familiar Isaiah passage:

> *I have called you by name, you are mine.*
> *When you pass through the waters, I will be with you;*
> *and through the rivers, they shall not overwhelm you. . . .*
> *You are precious in my sight,*
> *and honored, and I love you.*[58]

How personal, how intimate, how reassuring! How special to be addressed by one's name, to be known so well, remembered so personally, and welcomed so warmly. Loren has crossed many deep waters in the past several months, but he has not lost his confidence or trust in the promises of a loving, waiting, welcoming God.

---

[58] Isaiah 43:1–2

Although Loren knows everyone who comes into his bedroom, he is not having extended conversations; his talk deals more with the essentials. His patient, gentle, loving spirit, however, continues to shine through his frail and weakened body.

Friday, January 29, 2010

The daily pattern for Loren of late has been sleeping through the night (most nights); awakening in the morning for medications, morning freshening, and turning; and soon after that exertion sleeps soundly until mid to late afternoon. At this time he gets clear as to time, day, and date and then is usually awake until he prepares for the night's rest.

Late this afternoon Mary invited her father to talk about his past work, events, experiences, and interesting people in his life. Although his voice was weak, he was strong on remembering the details and articulating some of the interesting details from his past. These conversations have been opportunities to share events with the family from the past that they were perhaps unaware of or unfamiliar with, and it is an interesting recall for me. In the midst of sharing these stories, he exclaimed, "Wouldn't it be wonderful if I could die while telling the story of my hopes for the future?"

Life continues for Loren. Physiologically, we wonder how it can. Just last evening Loren said he would like to die in his sleep. He prayed a version of the childhood prayer, "For it is in my sleep that I pray the Lord my soul will take, and that precisely is my prayer now." We, his family, also offer this prayer for Loren.

Saturday, January 30, 2010

Loren was delighted with a visit from a couple whose friendship has spanned some 45 years. He described the visit as "heavenly—and I mean heavenly." No one is an island unto himself or herself. All phases of life require and benefit from community in order to function to the full extent of our ability and potential. We need each other. As it takes a village to raise a child, so also it takes a community to walk with a person who is dying. We have been the benefactors of such a community—family and friends both near and far continue to accompany us in this journey.

On our dining room table we have a bowl of flower bulbs sitting in water with rocks, sprouting roots, and green shoots. Since there is no soil, nourishment comes from the bulb itself. Similarly, with food intake having been almost nil for Loren these past couple of months or more, he is drawing from his stored reserves to keep his body going and mind active. He remains content and grateful.

Tonight I would like to close with a quote from Albert Einstein, printed on a beautiful card we received that says it all, "The most beautiful thing we can experience is the mysterious."

Sunday, January 31, 2010

This morning after church I visited with two musician friends. They will be performing a recital together in February. The one musician mentioned he will be playing a Bach cantata (BWV 82) entitled, *Ich Habe Genug (I Have Enough).* He said the words in this beautiful work caused him to think of Loren. After returning home, we found the words on the Internet. When I read these words to Loren, he was deeply moved and said how clearly these words express his sentiments and asked that I send them out as our evening CaringBridge entry.

This work was first performed on February 2, 1727, in Leipzig, Germany. The poet is unknown.

I have now enough,
I have now my Savior, the hope of the faithful.
Within my desiring embrace now enfolded;
I have now enough!
On him have I gazed,
My faith now hath Jesus impressed on my heart;
I would now, today yet, with gladness
Make hence my departure.
I have now enough. My hope is this alone.
That Jesus might belong to me and I to him.
In faith I hold to him, for I, too, see with Simeon
The gladness of that life beyond.
Let us in this man's burden join!

Ah! Would that from the bondage of my body
the Lord might free me. Ah! My departure, were it here,
With joy I'd say to thee, O world; I have now enough.
Slumber now, ye eyes so weary,
Fall in soft and calm repose!
World, I dwell no longer here,
Since I have no share in thee
Which my soul could offer comfort.
Here I must with sorrow reckon,
But yet, there, there I shall witness
Sweet repose and quiet rest.
My God! When comes that blessed "Now!"
When I in peace shall walk forever,
Both in the sand of earth's own coolness
And there within thy bosom rest?
My parting is achieved,
O world, good night
Rejoicing do I greet my death,
Ah, would that it had come already.
I'll escape then all the woe
Which doth here in the world confine me.

Monday, February 1, 2010

In contrast to previous days, Loren has been awake much of today. On such days time becomes long for him, particularly since he is confined to bed and is limited in strength and movement. At such times it becomes easy to become anxious, uneasy, and apprehensive.

We had a visit from the hospice nurse and a helpful discussion with her on things that can be done to help relieve the anxiety. Loren does acknowledge that at times he feels anxious and trapped. Acknowledging these feelings perhaps can be helpful in easing the angst. Medication is helpful and can give relief too, since the nurse said anxiety serves no useful purpose. Reassurance and encouragement are particularly important during these times.

Mark checked out several DVDs on travel and history at the public library, which Loren enjoys. Loren has been watching one this evening, enjoying it, and feeling more relaxed. Granddaughter Siri came and will spend the night with us.

Borrowing from Julian of Norwich, we pray "in the certainty that all is well, that all shall be well, and all manner of things will be well, for all rest in You."

Tuesday, February 2, 2010

Today Loren has had visits from his sister and dear friends with whom we have shared so much over the decades. He has slept more today, with his engagements with visitors remaining short, yet much appreciated. He has not been as troubled with anxiety as he was yesterday. Of late, each day has been much the same, yet each day is also different. There is no predictability or preciseness in this mystery of dying.

I know it has been a difficult journey for Loren, but I remain most grateful that he continues to remain gentle, kind, and grateful. He has not been bitter or angry, although he does want to question God's timing in his dying process. His greatest challenge, when awake, is restlessness and moments of anxiety. He especially appreciates a family member who can sit with him and hold his hand at these times.

Our talks together center most often on the many blessings we have known and shared together with our family, good friends, colleagues, and each other. Although I know our parting will be very sad, Loren and I remain forever grateful for our rich life together.

Wednesday, February 3, 2010

Another rather quiet day. With the exception of his morning's bath given by the home health aide, Loren slept much of the day until late afternoon. When awake he says he feels very weak and tired. Loren does not often complain of pain; fortunately, that is managed well with regular medication.

In addition to the home health aide visit, Loren had a visit from the hospice chaplain and several family members. Some of the visits were short as he was very tired, but the visits were all appreciated.

Long and uncertain times of waiting become an exercise in patience. Patience does not come easily to most of us; however, even this challenge can become a growing and learning experience for each of us.

Thursday, February 4, 2010

Recently, we have had the experience of Loren going from being almost totally unresponsive to being completely engaged and lucid within a 24-hour period. At moments we have felt like death was near, only to be totally surprised a few hours later, when Loren becomes fully alert and present to us again. Some days feel like a roller coaster. This ability of the human body to respond and continue in the face of so much frailty and weakness is beyond our understanding. It seems that Loren still has many surprises for us! There seems to be an incredible store of spiritual, physical, and emotional reserve that is being called forth and drawn upon in these days.

Today we had a dear friend come and simply sit with Loren and hold his hand in wordless conversation and prayer. What a gift! Our pastor also stopped by this afternoon for a visit with Loren, although he was unable to communicate much with her.

We are very grateful for the love and caring gestures and kindnesses that come our way. They are all appreciated and very helpful when often there is neither time nor energy to attend to all the needs of the day.

Friday, February 5, 2010

Today was another day of mixed experiences. If one looked at only one snippet of the day, it would not tell the full story. There are times Dad is too weak to talk or swallow. Hours later he may be asking for a drink and talking with more energy. Overall, he seems weaker each day, and today he had times of confusion. Yet, in his confusion, he is always wondering how things work, what the possible agenda might be, and how we might get the word to everyone about something he feels is very important.

This afternoon when Dad asked what we could do, he decided he wanted me to read to him. I began reading Greg Mortenson's book *Stones into Schools: Promoting Peace with Books, Not Bombs, in Afghanistan and Pakistan*. When we took a break from reading, he said he wanted to try to read himself, so we put his glasses on and set the book up in his bed, and he gazed at the book awhile before he said that it wasn't working for him to read. (This snippet of seeing him in bed with a book and his reading glasses on contrasts to earlier in the day.) In reading the book's introduction, I was struck by Mortenson's description of the time and patience required in the building of each school. The first school was finished in 1999. Before construction could begin, a suspension bridge needed to be built to carry the supplies across a deep gorge. Mortenson describes how each school requires some sort of bridge, "not necessarily a physical structure, but a span of emotional links that are forged over many years and many shared cups of tea. . . . As any wise village elder will tell you, anything truly important is worth doing very, *very* slowly."[59] While our time frame is much different than building a school in remote villages, the words were comforting.

We continue to try to create emotional links for Dad as he lingers in his dying. And yet we also know how truly important it is to be with him during this process.

~ *Becky (child #4)*

Saturday, February 6, 2010

A quote by Teilhard de Chardin[60] I received from a friend today expresses well what we pray we can be attentive to these days of watching and waiting with Loren: "Above all, trust in the slow work of God."

Sunday, February 7, 2010

As we think of today's Bible text of the fisherpeople being encouraged to move out into deeper waters, I thought about the journey Loren is making now. He is moving out into deeper waters, and that can be calm and peaceful, as well as challenging and fearful. Today we have seen more troubled waters for Loren. He has acknowledged that dying is hard and that he is discouraged but not fearful. As Mary and I were preparing him for the night, he asked for water. The real water did not seem to satisfy him; Mary marked his forehead with water, reminding him of his baptism. After that he kept referring to "water in a shell": "Get a shell—water in a shell." I found a shell and poured

---

[59] Page 18

[60] Pierre Teilhard de Chardin, French philosopher, Jesuit priest, and scientist

water into it. This seemed to please him. He drank from the shell, and Mary and I sang, *Shall We Gather at the River?* After drinking from the shell, he was satisfied. Then he said, "This gives life." This homemade ritual was sacred for us—it was worship. Yes, it was our evening worship.

Monday, February 8, 2010

This has been a difficult day for Loren and an emotional day for us. It seems that the physical, psychological, and spiritual are all blending together and are being integrated. Loren has complained of more physical pain, as well as having times of anxiety and restlessness, as well as deep sleep. Water has been a focus for him again today—holding water, drinking water, and later today, refusing water. We feel Loren is detaching himself more and more from this world.

His voice is weak and oftentimes difficult to discern. His comments are usually one or two words, leaving us with the mystery of what he really wants to say or what the background is for his comment.

This afternoon he refused the bath and care from the home health aide, which he normally enjoys so much. Later he also refused a medication. When Paul asked if he should stay with him, he responded, "No, I want to be with God."

This evening we sang around his bed, and that seemed calming for him. Later while Paul was sitting with him as he was going to sleep, he murmured, "I know what is happening." A few moments later, "It's too much!" and repeated this phrase several times.

We pray for a peaceful rest for him this night.

Tuesday, February 9, 2010

We have watched and waited with Loren today as he has slipped into a coma and remains unresponsive to us. We had a timely visit from the hospice nurse this evening, and she confirmed that Loren shows signs of approaching death. She helped us to understand what to be aware of at this time and how best to attend to these developments. Loren is being kept as comfortable as possible.

We have spoken personal words to him today, and we have sung to him, believing that at some level he is hearing us.

I end my entry this evening with this quote from our hospice handbook: "The transition from life can be every bit as profound, intimate and precious as the miracle of birth." *Ira R. Byock*

Wednesday, February 10, 2010

The waiting continues, with Loren sleeping all night and day, until late this afternoon, when he opened his eyes. He did not speak and did not seem able to do so. It appeared that his awaking was triggered by pain, which we were finally able to discern by asking him to raise a finger if he was in pain, which he did. After receiving pain medications, his eyes remained open, with a glassy distant stare. At times it seemed he tried to say something, but we were unable to discern what it was. His eyes were open for a period of time, and then he fell into a deep sleep again.

Today we had helpful visits from the hospice nurse and our pastor. The entire family gathered for a supper of homemade soup and bread prepared by Becky.

The words we shared with Loren today have been whispered words of our love for him and our release of him into the waiting arms of a loving God.

Thursday, February 11, 2010

Softly playing in Loren's bedroom this morning and evening and wafting throughout the apartment was the calming, repetitive, beautiful instrumental Taizé music. How soothing and comforting it was for us, and I hope it was for Loren, as well, as he slept. He slept the night and has been in a deep sleep all day. His steady breathing has sounded like the ocean waves, as Lisa suggested. We see physical signs of his life ebbing away; however, he appears to be at peace and comfortable.

Friday, February 12, 2010

Loren has remained in continuous deep sleep. Breathing is slowed at times, regular at times, and at times he has periods of apnea. He was tended by his regular home health aide and visited by the hospice nurse today but has not responded to either care or touch. He has not shown any signs of discomfort or pain, which can be detected by facial grimacing, furrowed brow, or restlessness.

The family comes and goes, giving tender care and comfort to Loren and invaluable support and help to me. I am grateful that we have been able to honor Loren's wishes to be cared for in our home during his illness and to die at home. This would not have been possible without the continuous rotation of help from everyone in our family.

And so we pray for a peaceful transition for Loren into the welcoming arms of our gracious and loving God.

Saturday, February 13, 2010

We have not seen much change in Loren's condition today from yesterday. He is in a deep sleep all the time now and remains unresponsive. His body appears to be incredibly strong and resilient, considering his frail condition and lack of food for many weeks and now lack of water also in the past several days. The body is complex, wonderful, and mysterious! We continue to whisper our love for him and our release of him to his final rest.

Sunday, February 14, 2010

The steady rise and fall of deep breathing has filled our apartment like a sacred mantra these past several days. The first breath Loren drew began life for him, and now these days we await and pray for the beginning of another life, a new life, for Loren.

Breathe on Loren, breath of God,
Fill him with life anew,
Breathe on Loren breath of God,
So he shall never die,
But live with you the perfect life
For all eternity.

(Adapted from the old hymn "Breathe on Me, Breath of God")

Monday, February 15, 2010

My beloved Loren died at 2:00 this afternoon. All the children were present—the last one arriving only 15 minutes before he died. The last words spoken to Loren by Paul were, "Mom, Paul, Mark, Mary, Becky, and Joel are all here. May you go in peace. It's okay for you to go."

The hospice nurse had just been here and was still in the building when Loren died. She was able to come up and take care of all the arrangements. She was also able to remove Loren's wedding band that I now wear as a necklace. This was my promise to Loren that this was one of the ways we would stay connected.

Pastor Susan was present for a sending ritual around Loren's bed, together with the extended family.

Individual responses were shared, and we concluded with singing the ARC blessing: "May the longtime sun shine upon you, all love surround you, and the pure light within you guide you on your way home."

Loren had requested that his body be donated to the University of Minnesota anatomy bequest program for research. This is fitting for who he was, and this gift of his body will allow his teaching to continue.

I am very grateful to the Fairview Hospice staff who have walked with us these past three and one half months, giving support, counsel, and professional help. I am also grateful for the support and encouragement we have received from this CaringBridge site.

I will close this entry with some reflections I wrote about my life with Loren.

> *Loren, what I will always cherish and be grateful for is:*
> *Your patient, kind manner,*
> *Your acceptance of your illness and impending death,*
> *Your deep love for your spouse and your family*
> *Your fun-loving playfulness with children and grandchildren,*
> *Your thoughtfulness in your responses,*
> *Your gentleness in relating to everyone who comes into our home,*
> *Your sharp wit and ever-ready humor,*
> *Your storytelling ability,*

Your curiosity regarding solutions to issues and problems,
Your dedication to and concern for the poor and marginalized,
Your ongoing love of learning,
Your keen memory of past events,
Your ability to write creatively and compellingly,
Your ability to dream, create, and color outside the lines,
Your openness to change and your ability to change,
Your delight in creating surprises for your spouse,
Your progressive and innovative ideas,
Your ability to network with people,
Your commitment to justice and peace efforts,
Your support of the GLBT community,
Your certainty and thankfulness for the inclusive and unconditional love of God,
Your faithful love and partnership for over 57 and one half years!
A heart filled with gratitude,
Your Ruthie

"Death is not extinguishing the light. It is putting out the lamp because the dawn has come." —*Rabindranath Tagore*[61]

In the fullness of this time, I close with both gratitude and grief,

~ *Ruth*

---

[61] Indian/Bengali poet and mystic, and the first non-European winner of the Nobel Prize for literature, in 1913

Tuesday, February 16, 2010

Sleep did not come easily to me or to other members of our family last night. It was difficult to take in the full truth that the physical presence of Loren is no longer with us. Today we are just beginning to feel the accumulated tiredness we have not let ourselves feel before. I realize that this new process of grieving will take time and attention as well.

The many expressions of your love and care are greatly appreciated.

Wednesday, February 17, 2010

There are moments in the day when grief wants to take over, and there are moments when all is well. These days are filled with preparation details for Loren's Celebration of Life service[62] and attending to the many other particulars following a death. Being surrounded by family and being kept occupied with necessary matters now seems to lessen or perhaps postpone the rawness of grief and separation. The grieving process will be another learning experience and will take time. I know that I am not alone, that I am surrounded by many loving friends, neighbors, and family and certainly by a compassionate and loving God.

Yes, I feel suspended in grace and held in love!

---

[62] The service was held on February 20 at 2:00 p.m. at Gloria Dei Lutheran Church in Saint Paul.

Thursday, February 18, 2010

Madeleine L'Engle[63] said something like this when she wrote about the death of her husband: the price of deep love is deep loss. That expresses well my feelings at this time. I am very grateful for the many years Loren and I were granted together, yet the physical separation is difficult now and will be in the days ahead. We did so much together and shared many of the same interests and even partnered in some of our work. When you reach the point where you finish each other's sentences, come up with the same ideas or the same thoughts at the same time, you know you have been deeply enmeshed in each other's lives for a long time. This was true for Loren and me. I am grateful for the years we shared. At this time of profound loss, I thank God for the gift of enduring love.

Friday, February 19, 2010,

Last November Loren was asked to give the sermon at the church[64] where he was baptized, confirmed, and ordained. Later our family attended this church, and now Becky and Dan and family worship there. As I reflected on what I could write on the eve of Loren's Celebration of Life service, I thought of his sermon that was titled, "Is the End the Beginning?"[65] Since Loren was too ill to deliver the sermon, Dan agreed to preach it on his behalf. Now Loren knows in full and is

---

[63] American novelist and author of such children's classics as *A Wrinkle in Time* and *Many Waters*

[64] University Lutheran Church of Hope, Minneapolis

[65] See appendix B for full sermon.

fully known. His questions are answered, the mystery is revealed, and all things have become new. Death leads to transformation and new life. Yes, I dare to believe that he is beginning something new, something beautiful, something wonderful.

Saturday, February 20, 2010

Our time of watching and waiting with Loren ended five days ago. We arrived home this evening, filled with immense thanksgiving for a day that honored Loren's life and ministry. The Celebration of Life service was a deep and profound worship experience beginning with the "remembrance of our baptism." It included extraordinary music from combined choirs, instrumentalists, rousing congregational singing, heartfelt tributes, and selected scriptural readings from Isaiah, James, and the Gospel of Luke. We concluded by celebrating the Eucharist. It was a beautiful and sacred day for me, our family, and our many friends from near and far, a day full of grace.

With love,
~ *Ruth and family*

Sunday, February 21, 2010

I continue to receive an outpouring of love, care, and support from our immediate family; our extended family who have traveled here from Norway, Alaska, Boston, North Dakota, Illinois, and closer geographic points; the Becketwood community; the ARC community; and a host of other friends. I cannot adequately express how important your support has been to my family and me. These past two days have been filled with celebration, joy, remembrances, waves of grief, and making connections with so many.

Yesterday morning began with making final arrangements for the wonderful Celebration of Life service for Loren held at Gloria Dei Church. Afterward the celebration continued with family gatherings and many conversations. The time will soon come when I will be alone, and I am preparing to enter this phase of grieving. I was gratified to learn that the Fairview Hospice program conducts a 13-month grief and support group for surviving members of hospice patients who have died.

Death is a part of life. However, there will be adjustments in not having the bodily presence of someone with whom so much as been shared for so long. I do not face the future with fear. However, I can imagine there will be days of deep loneliness and emptiness. I will try to walk through these times with trust and confidence remembering that I am really not alone.

This will be my last journal entry on this site now that Loren's earthly journey is over. I thank you all for your encouraging, supportive, and oftentimes profound guestbook entries and for the many connections made through the CaringBridge site. What a tremendous service this has been! I offer my gratitude for your accompaniment on this difficult, beautiful, tender, and holy time. I have learned much and received much.

“Death is not extinguishing the light; it is only putting out the lamp because the dawn has come.”

Appendix B

"Is the End the Beginning?"

Sermon and Poem by Loren E. Halvorson, as Read by Dan O'Loughlin

When the daily news is a cacophony of bad news—corruption, conflict, crises, and confusion—do we need texts about catastrophes, despair, death?[1] When things are so bad, should we not put the best face possible on them? Should not the church year conclude with the "Hallelujah" chorus, fireworks displays, celebration? We don't come to church to be depressed, do we?

This Sunday I suspect many preachers are tempted to look for happier texts, ones that anesthetize the congregation and escape reality with synthetic reality. Entertain instead

---

[1] The Gospel reading for this date was Mark 13:1–8, in which Jesus describes for his followers the turmoil before "the end" comes.

of engage, forget rather than remember. There is a whole industry out there helping us to escape. During the last days of the Roman Empire, citizens were herded into the coliseums to be entertained by violence—gory battles between humans and beasts—while the empire was crumbling from corruption within and being destroyed by barbarians from without.

Perhaps we need such texts to have our cages rattled, our false securities revealed, our agendas challenged, our insanity exposed—to reverse way, to change, to repent. When you are at the end of exhaling, you need to reverse direction, as we know from the life-sustaining exercise of breathing. And so the seasons of the year teach us: after months of productivity, a rest, a retreat, a 180-degree turn to right the imbalance.

But I think there is a deeper mystery here beyond the symmetry of living. And that is the role of darkness in exposing the hope that is hidden in darkness, of the mystery that an end can be a beginning, that the point of breakdown may be the point of breaking open. In the mystic tradition, it is called "the dark night of the soul."

When you look into the role that darkness plays in the shaping of the human soul, you get a glimpse of something unusual going on. A complete reversal of the way we imagine things to be. Ends become beginnings, no's are transformed into yeses. Despair into delight, death into life. Do we miss the good news because we will not face the bad news—about ourselves, our generation, our nation?

The comfort that Scripture brings is packaged in bad news. Hope is hidden in helplessness, joy in judgment, promise in paradox. Death in the Christian faith does not lead to termination but to transformation. The doctors have told me that cancer will soon end my life, but that very news has generated new life. Ruth and I decided to make the most of the days that are left by celebrating friendships, inviting old acquaintances over for "three cups of tea," and to live more fully and intentionally, not to escape reality but to experience the deeper reality of a richer life. God's grace is a mischievous and surprising matter. Not at all what we expected. Is the secret in learning how to live, learning how to die?

Is this what Jesus meant when he said that you find your life by losing it? Life begins with the last chapter. In the story of our life, it's okay to read the last chapter first. Truth-telling is a terror to the ego. When you are at the end of the line, you see where you need to go. The Gospel has a way of upsetting properly ordered things. Of course this doesn't make sense until you view life from the end, for that's the starting point. Confession precedes profession. No precedes yes, but it is not the final word. Yes is the ultimate word, and the ultimate word trumps the penultimate word. The end of the story defines the story itself. That is why we keep stories of the end of life in the pericope [biblical texts].

Life begins with pain. The valley of the shadow of death can be a birth canal; the dark night of the soul, the womb where life begins again and again. And here is where the feminine image of God with a womb creates new life out of excruciating pain and great suffering (whether in the manger or the cross), something that many souls who have anguished and languished in the night hours know.

There is a book in German that contains letters from people on death row in Nazi prisons because they opposed fascism. It is entitled [in English], *You Visited Me in the Night*. The title comes from Psalm 17:3,[2] which I can now understand much better while struggling with my own imminent death from cancer. God has visited me in the night and I know that the pain of death is the threshold for a new, unimaginable life.

---

[2] "If you try my heart, if you visit me by night, / if you test me, you will find no wickedness in me; / my mouth does not transgress."

There is an old story of two monks who debated for years what heaven would be like. They made a covenant that whoever died first would seek to communicate back to his friend on earth what heaven is really like. They were not sure how this could be communicated, so they devised a code of two Latin words: *funditus*, to say whether heaven was all that they expected; or *alitus*, totally different from what they expected. After one of the monks died, the other waited daily for an answer whether it would be *funditus* (what they expected) or *alitus* (totally different). One day in the garden he heard a small voice that sounded like his friend saying "*funditus alitus, funditus alitus*" ("totally other").

Oh it's a surprise all right, a big one. Hope drives out all fear. This is why I believe when God approaches humans, as Jesus did after his resurrection, he uses the preemptive-strike words, "Do not be afraid." Fear is trumped by faith. The opposite of faith is not doubt but certitude—the certitude proclaimed loudly on the airwaves today by bloggers who are, I believe, driven by fear. We need not fear these dreaded texts at the end of the church year, for embedded in them is the promise of a new creation where "all things are made new," an incomprehensible yes hidden in the harsh no. Here lies the answer to the debate that has haunted Lutherans about how the law is related to the Gospel, how the God of judgment can at the same time be the God of grace.

The word *confession* has this double, paradoxical meaning of (1) repentance of sins and (2) the confidence of forgiveness. This truth has transformed many a dark night of death into the brilliant morning of resurrection, turned the anguish of feeling forsaken on a cross to the unrestrained joy of an empty tomb. Death does not destroy life but paradoxically births it. The purpose of these frightening and irksome texts at the end of the liturgical year is, I believe, to convey this seemingly contradictory truth. We do not need to avoid them, gloss over them, but plunge right into them and unpackage the incredible hope that is there. Do not be afraid of death that takes your breath away totally, for it brings everything you hoped for . . . and more.

[Addendum by the sermon's reader, Dan O'Loughlin] I end with the poem my father-in-law [Loren] wrote three weeks ago, entitled "God Spoke to Me."

God spoke to me the other day,
a woman's voice, God's not just a "he."
It was a surprising experience,
sounded just like my wife, Ruthie.
Later God said, "I love you,"
this time in a masculine voice.
I'd swear was our oldest son.
It seems that God can make that choice.
God kissed me the other day,
right on the lips intimately;
and you know what it really felt like?
Like my great-granddaughter Lucy.
God did promise to live right here in us,
which is not very far away;
you know the neat thing about that?
You can be with God every day.
"Got some time next week?" I asked.
It's fun talking with the Deity.
"Got all the time in the world" said God.
"How about an eternity?"

Appendix C

Halvorson Obituary, Minneapolis Star Tribune, *February 17, 2010*

Halvorson enabled laity to do church's work

The pastor, teacher, theologian and author taught at Luther Seminary and co-founded the ARC Retreat Center near Cambridge, Minn.

by TIM HARLOW

The Rev. Loren Halvorson arrived in [Germany] four years after World War II to find buildings still lying in ruin and scores of people living in abject poverty.

The grisly scene was the starting point of his ministry, dedicated to empowering the laity and the disenfranchised and to championing the causes of social ethics and human rights as a pastor, teacher, theologian and author.

"That was a major shaper of his life and ministry," said his daughter, the Rev. Mary Halvorson, pastor at Grace University Lutheran Church in Minneapolis.

Loren Halvorson died of prostate cancer Monday at Becketwood Cooperative in Minneapolis. He was 82.

In 1949, he helped Latvian and other Baltic refugees find homes in the United States and other countries as a resettlement representative for Lutheran World Federation. Spurred by the lay movement taking place in 1950s Germany, Halvorson went on to become a progressive voice encouraging the faithful to actively carry out the mission of the church, those who knew him said.

Believing the church is not a hierarchal institution, but rather small assemblies of people equipped to do its work, Halvorson led town meetings throughout Minnesota in the 1960s in which he brought politicians, citizens and others together to talk about faith and its impact.

From 1959 to 1992, Halvorson was a professor of church and society at Luther Seminary in St. Paul, where he used his wit, spontaneity, vision and vast knowledge to teach students to have open minds. He also taught at United Theological Seminary in New Brighton.

"His lectures were filled with testimonies from people such as Desmond Tutu," and he taught students to be "open to voices that are often dismissed and understand those who come from different backgrounds," said Paul Sponheim, professor emeritus at Luther Seminary.

Halvorson teamed with his wife, Ruth, to found the ARC Retreat center near Cambridge, Minn.

Halvorson wrote three books, "Grace at Point Zero," "Peace on Earth Handbook" and "Exodus into the World."

In addition to his wife and daughter, Halvorson is survived by three sons, Paul, Mark and Joel, all of Minneapolis; another daughter, Becky Halvorson of Minneapolis; two sisters, Gayle Mosand of Norway, and Betty Caspar of Minneapolis; seven grandchildren; and two great-grandchildren.[1]

Text Acknowledgments

The scriptural quotations contained herein are from the New Revised Standard Version Bible, copyright © 1989 by the Division of Christian Education of the National Council of the Churches of Christ in the United States of America. All rights reserved.

The quotation on page vii is excerpted from E. B. White, "Some Remarks on Humor," in *Essays of E. B. White* (New York: McGraw-Hill Humanities/Social Sciences/Languages, 2000), 308.

The quotation on page 15 is excerpted from Richard Rohr, *Radical Grace: Daily Meditations* (New York: St. Anthony Messenger Press, 1995), 154.

The quotation on page 16 is Proverb XXIX, excerpted from Antonio Machado, *There Is No Road: Proverbs by Antonio Machado*, Dennis Maloney, ed., transl. by Mary Berg (Buffalo, NY: White Pines, 2003).

The quotation on pages 29 and 108 is excerpted from *Out of the Ordinary: Prayers, Poems and Reflections for Every Season*, by Joyce Rupp. Copyright 2011 by Ave Maria Press, P.O. Box 428, Notre Dame, IN 46556. Used with permission of the publisher.

The quotation on page 34 is excerpted from Rainer Maria Rilke, *Letters to a Young Poet*, transl. by M. D. Herter (New York, London: Norton, 1954), 27.

The poem on page 40 is from William Blake, *The Poetical Works of William Blake*, John Sampson, ed. (London, New York: Oxford University Press, 1908).

The hymn verse on page 46 is excerpted from Stephen Paulus and Michael Dennis Browne, "Pilgrim's Hymn" (Saint Paul: Paulus Publications, 1997).

The quotation on page 51 is excerpted from James E. Miller, *Winter Grief, Summer Grace* (Minneapolis: Augsburg Fortress, 1995), 57. Used by permission.

The quotation on page 53 is excerpted from Henri J. M. Nouwen, *Here and Now: Living in the Spirit* (New York: Crossroad Publishing 1994), 29.

The quotation on page 57 is excerpted from Anne Lamott, *Traveling Mercies: Some Thoughts on Faith* (New York: Pantheon, 1999), 143.

Grateful acknowledgment is extended to the Henri Nouwen Legacy Trust, 10 Montcrest Boulevard, Toronto, ON M4K 1J7, Canada, for permission to use the quotation on pages 57 and 98, excerpted from "All Is Grace," by Henri Nouwen, *Weavings*, vol. VII, no. 6 (November/December), 1992, 38. Used with permission.

The quotation on page 127 is excerpted from Frederick Buechner, *Secrets in the Dark* (New York: HarperCollins, 2006), 172–173.

The hymn verse on page 131 is excerpted from Ken Bible and F. Seguin, "Love Has Come" (Integrity's Hosanna! Music, 1996, in *Evangelical Book of Worship*, Minneapolis: Augsburg Fortress, 2006).

The quotation on pages 159–160 is excerpted from Greg Mortenson, *Stones into Schools: Promoting Peace with Education, Not Bombs, in Afghanistan and Pakistan* (New York: Penguin, 2009), 18.

Photo Acknowledgments

Cover: hardcover, © iStockPhoto/Nikada; softcover, © iStockPhoto.com/IakovKalinin and © iStockPhoto.com/Nikada

Page 9: Road to the ARC retreat center. Photo courtesy of ARC.

Page 31: "Hands" copyright © 2009 by Jonathan Halvorson Frissell.

Page 49: Cross-stitch embroidery by Loren Halvorson. Photo copyright © 2013 by Mark Halvorson.

Page 63: Memorial stones at the ARC retreat center. Photo courtesy of ARC.

Page 65: "Birches," painting by Harry Nurmet, copyright © 1984 by Harry Nurmet. Used by permission of Märt Nurmet. Photo copyright © 2013 by Mark Halvorson.

Page 165: Loren Halvorson portrait, copyright © by Ruth Halvorson.